SNAP & GO

URGENCY, DISCIPLINE, AND
FINISHING THROUGH THE WHISTLE

JACK HARNEDY

STREAMLINE
BOOKS

PRAISE FOR SNAP & GO

In my time working with Jack, he was and continues to be an inspirational leader, drawing essential business and life lessons from his time in the trenches as a member of the Northwestern Wildcats O-line. These lessons were essential to forming, shaping, and advancing our business culture on the team and spoke loud and clear to the concepts of servant leadership, practicing and preparation (not just showing up in "game day"), and standing together in the trenches to accomplish team goals which were wildly more important than personal goals. To this day these lessons ring true in the foundation of my leadership work with the teams I have had the privilege of leading since working with and for Jack.

— Tom Choi, Vice President, The Kellogg Company

I have enjoyed the good fortune of working with Jack Harnedy as a sports marketing client for the past 10 years. He quickly became more than a client but also a colleague, friend, and even a mentor. His peaceful, easy and outgoing personality that draws you in, belies the underlying focus and intensity that make him a winner in business and in life. Snap and Go is a gift to us all from one of the great friends, fathers, and business leaders of our time.

— Tad Geschickter, Owner of JTG Daugherty Racing

In business and in life there are so many correlations with sports, especially when it comes to teamwork, competition and preparedness. Jack seamlessly brings this to life through his authentic voice and real-life stories, in his quest to make every day count.

— Christina Groth, Vice President Merchandising, The Kroger Company

Whoa Jackie Boy…can't wait to include this Snap & Go mentality in my talks…especially with my grandkids…

— Gary Barnett, former Northwestern Wildcats Head Football Coach

Snap & Go is the perfect resource for individuals who want to take their leadership to the next level. I highly recommend this book!

— Alex Demczak, Bestselling author of The Sale and Thrive U

To Erin, Alec & Elise.

*For your love, encouragement, and support,
everyday.*

*You are my source of energy and my everything.
My drive is all for you.*

1

There is a motion that comes as naturally to me as drinking water or taking a bite of food. It is a motion I could "do in my sleep" (as they say) and comfortably conduct with my eyes closed. The motion involves standing with legs spread wide apart, while bent forward — standing over a prolate spheroid shape of brown leather. Did you know that's the technical term for the shape of a football? A prolate spheroid. Kind of a weird term. And this is kind of a weird "motion" that I have down to a "T."

However, unlike drinking or eating, this specific motion wasn't something I was born with. No, it is a motion that was more so ingrained into my being—something so embedded into my muscle memory that I could spread my legs apart today, bend over a football, and snap the football to a person standing 45 feet behind me with accuracy and precision.

This kind of feat may sound simple enough and, especially if you're not a football fan, quite meaningless. The art of snapping a football between one's legs with speed and accuracy isn't exactly a world-changing occurrence, but it is important when it comes to executing as a special teams unit. "Special teams" is the name given to the set of football players who handle on-field duties such as kickoffs, field goals, and punting. And throughout the majority of my childhood and young adult life, special teams were just part of my everyday routine.

Ten seconds. That's how long an average punt play lasts in any given football game. This number obviously depends on one of two factors: 1) if the punter kicks the ball out of bounds, and 2) if the punt *receiver* fields the ball and attempts to gain positive yardage on the play. Before I dive into too much football philosophy, I describe the average punt play for one reason: a long snapper's first priority is that first second. Or, more accurately, a long snapper's main goal is to deliver that football in *less than* a second. Whether in college or NFL, a quality "long snap" from the time the ball is flung backward to the hands of a punter, is between 0.6 and 0.7 seconds. The ball should typically travel between 35-40mph, and if it's not an accurate snap . . . the punter needs to either adjust his form to catch the ball and kick it downfield accordingly, or turn around and go chase a prolate spheroid as it bounces away from him in an unknown direction. Both of those scenarios are not ideal, and if a long snapper makes such a mistake, he will certainly have to answer for it on the sidelines afterward.

All of these numbers and circumstances and motions are things I'm quite familiar with because, from the time I was 5 years old, I began long snapping a football between my legs. It's not like my goal from birth was to make it to the NFL, but I did have a very special mentor who knew this specific motion could help in life later on. More on him in a bit.

For now, it's crucial that you know something else: my name isn't "long snapper." And I actually never made it to that NFL field to get a chance to snap a ball to an NFL punter. But I *did* perfect the motion in and throughout childhood, and I *did* have the opportunity to snap that funny leather ball on many NCAA Division I football fields across America.

My real name is Jack Harnedy. Not "long snapper." For a while, I had trouble differentiating the two. But that was many years ago, and I have since come into a stronger identity of myself and who I was born to be, and who I was born to do it alongside. I am married to my beautiful wife, Erin, and have two wonderful children, Alec and Elise. Those three individuals are, first and foremost, the most important people in my life. For many years, yes, the *punter* was one of the most important people to me—

because the punter is who I was in charge of delivering a football to at 35mph without an error in between.

The life I live today looks a little different than it did growing up playing the game I love. There is still a unique set of pressures and responsibilities I have today, but it obviously looks different than watching a bunch of special teams film on an upcoming opponent. What I will say is that, although different, there truly *is* a link between my upbringing and the life I live today. In fact, it's the core reason I had the idea to sit down and write the book you hold in your hands today.

Special teams and punting and football have their place in the discussion, yes, but there is so much more surrounding my life growing up that has had an effect on my current mindset, disciplines, and rhythms throughout daily life. These elements—mindset, discipline, rhythm—are at the core of what I consider to be a "goal" and takeaway for you after reading this book. It is wildly important for me to explain the background of such elements and their impact on my life because I believe that you might be able to glean something from these elements as well.

The "Snap & Go" Mentality

And so I'm led to the impetus for this book: to help instill a "Snap & Go" mentality in your life. It's obviously the title of this book, and it's the mentality that (beginning with the end in mind) I want to leave you with after you've finished reading.

Now, I'm aware that anytime someone hears "The (fill in the blank) Mentality" that one name typically comes to mind: Kobe Bryant. And yes, I know that Kobe is one of the greatest players to ever step on an NBA basketball court. His contribution and "Mamba Mentality" did so much for the game of basketball, and his legacy will live *far* beyond his untimely death in 2020. However, Kobe was not *the* best basketball player of all time.

That honor goes to a man who I spent years watching as a kid. A man who played basketball (essentially) right down the road from me, night after night, and mesmerized crowds every place he went. Michael Jordan is a once-in-a-generation kind of athlete and talent. Although he doesn't have a catchphrase like "Mamba Mentality" that encapsulates his on-court mindset, he does have a brand that is associated with just about any sport you can imagine—that brand is represented by his silhouette spread out for an "Air Jordan" dunk. And you've likely, at some point in life, wearing something with his logo on it.

Make no mistake, Michael Jordan knew about cultivating the proper mentality as an athlete. It's a mentality that any kid, such as myself, growing up in Chicago in the 1980s/1990s tried to emulate in his or her own little way. Some of us stuck our tongues out during pivotal in-game moments, and others took slight offenses in a personal way, using them for inspiration throughout a game or season. In speaking for my own teenage self, I truly resonated with the latter. MJ was obviously the best at this style of play, but I knew the power in it as well— even in high school. Many of us kinda knew about this philosophy—to a situation or circumstance and utilize it as motivation toward a common goal.

Which leads back to me. And yes, I'm aware . . . I'm not Kobe. I'm definitely not Michael. I'm Jack Harnedy, remember? Just an average kid from south side Chicago who grew up with a loving family and a wonderful surrounding community. What makes my story different from others? It's that I had a father who had some serious foresight.

Now, "foresight" is one way to put it. Looking back, I like to view it as a blend of circumstances that I was born into. Author Malcolm Gladwell, in his bestselling book *Outliers*, describes the following:

"Superstar lawyers and math whizzes and software entrepreneurs appear at first blush to lie outside ordinary experience. But they don't. They are products of history and community, of opportunity and legacy. Their success is not exceptional or mysterious. It is grounded in a web of advantages and inheritances, some deserved, some not, some earned, some just plain lucky--but all critical to making them who they are. The outlier, in the end, is not an outlier at all."

I can't really put it better than that. Similar to the quote, I am "a product of history and community, of opportunity and legacy." And guess what . . . so are you.

It just so happens that my community growing up was in a Chicago neighborhood, and part of my family history, somewhere along the line, contributed to a bigger physical frame that boded well within the rules of American football. But before I round out this chapter on the game of football and the Snap & Go mentality that I came to know and love, it's important to consider another definition of Gladwell's—a definition of success:

"Success is a function of persistence and doggedness and the willingness to work hard for twenty-two minutes to make sense of something that most people would give up on after thirty seconds."

That quote is almost as, if not more, important than the previous quote on outliers. Why? Because this quote on the definition of success should give anyone and everyone hope—no matter *where* they were born, *who* they knew growing up, or even *how old* they are today. All we can determine after birth, throughout childhood, and into adulthood is the amount of "persistence and doggedness and willingness" we're willing to put forth.

As for the numbers in that quote, Gladwell is essentially saying that many humans aren't willing to push through the first 30-seconds of something (if they're bad at it or it doesn't come naturally) before experiencing the benefits of sticking with it for some time. Growing up, for me, I don't need to think long about what took me a while to learn but paid off in the end . . .

Long-snapping a football is one of the funniest things to watch someone do—especially if it's his or her first try. To reiterate from before, you spread your legs apart, extending beyond shoulder-width, lean over the (aforementioned) prolate spheroid, grip the football itself (with a specific grip that *does* matter), and fling the thing between your legs to someone standing 45 feet behind you. "Precision" is the word, and enacting this motion *with* precision takes way longer than 30 seconds or 22 minutes to perfect.

It's a funny motion to watch someone else do, but it's *also* a funny feeling to try for yourself. I'd encourage you, if you haven't ever before in your life, to find the nearest prolate spheroid you can, and go through the steps listed above. You might need to find someone who will catch the ball for you on the receiving end, but you can take turns long-snapping to each other.

As for my "long-snapping" buddy? Well, I have a man by the name of Jack Harnedy. A man that many in our community knew as *Coach* Harnedy. But I am lucky enough to have called him "Dad."

Yes, much more than my "long-snapping buddy" was someone who showed me the skill when I had only been walking for a few years. I was maybe four or five when I recall performing this long-snapping motion for the first time. I'm sure Dad got a kick out of it — like I said, watching someone do it for the first time is comical in itself . . . I know watching a five-year-old perform the motion brings a unique blend of comedy and cute. But to me, even as a kid, I never thought it was "cute." I thought it was cool. You see, the reason my Dad (read: Jack) was also called "Coach" is because he actually did serve as an assistant coach for the freshman and sophomore football teams at Mount Carmel High School — for 16 years or so.

And for about 10 of those years, I grew up idolizing the young men on Dad's teams and pretty much everything that surrounded high school football. As a young kid, those kinds of teams might as well consist of NFL players walking around . . . that's how much I looked up to many of them. And I know other coaches' sons and daughters can say the same if they grew up around their parents' high school or college teams.

So there I was, long-snapping a football between my legs as a child. A few of the players on Dad's teams would, throughout the years, teach me a thing or two to help me perfect the motion. I just thought it was awesome *whenever* those guys acknowledged me, but helping me hone in on a particular skill was exciting . . . especially when I started getting really good at long-snapping. Now, my Dad was well aware that this one particular skill, if perfected, would increase any young man's odds of playing football at the next level—be it high school, college, or potentially the NFL. We had conversations about that growing up, and his logic always made sense to me.

Here's what I had yet to realize as a kid growing up: the skill of snapping a football between one's legs was just the first part of the play.

Yep, it's maybe the "obvious" point I haven't brought up until now, but the 0.6 seconds it takes to snap a football back to the punter is *literally* just a fraction of what happens on a punting play in the game of football. What comes next? Here's one way to put it: 10 seconds of chaos.

That is to say . . . if the punter kicks a ball that 1) stays in bounds, 2) is fielded by the punt returner, and 3) is *returned* by the punt returner. Those three steps, after the prolate spheroid is snapped by the long-snapper (such as myself) and kicked by the punter, are what comprise the *other* seconds of this wild play in football. So, for all intents and purposes, let's assume, for the duration of this book, that when I refer to a "Snap &

Go" mentality, I'm talking about the play as a whole . . .

1. Practice throughout the week prior.

2. Visualize yourself playing in the game.

3. Focus during pre-game.

4. Line up accordingly.

5. Scan the defense.

6. Look back at the punter to confirm he's ready.

7. Snap the ball.

8. Block a speedster rushing your gap.

9. Sprint downfield with your head on a swivel.

10. Locate and tackle the ball carrier.

A simple 10-step formula? Not a chance. It really *does* feel like chaos when enacted from start to finish. But I'll also tell you this: it's maybe the most exhilarating 10 seconds you could ever experience. (Outside of skydiving, which I can attest to firsthand).

Snap & Go is the result of me performing that 10-step process within the game of football, yes, but it also translated (and translates) into the way I have lived my entire life. For 40+ years, I took the disciplines and skill set involved with this one play and learned to gain an education, earn a job, start a family, build a career, and so much more. And lucky for me, I have had some incredible people along the way to aid me in that Snap & Go mentality.

The reason the "people" portion of that equation is so important is that people, in this short life we've been given, are *everything* in regard to the person we are today and the person we will become tomorrow.

With all that being said, welcome to my Snap & Go experience in life. It's 10 chapters long that represents 10 seconds on an average punt play. You will read about the people that made me along the way, and you'll learn how one single play in football impacted the life I live today. Why structure the book in this way? Because it is my belief, if we all captured a little more Snap & Go mentality in each of our lives, our world would be a different place. But it has to start with one person, and I hope that person is you.

I promise not to laugh the first time you snap a ball through your legs. I'm pretty sure I looked hilarious the first time I tried to do it. Then again . . . I was five.

2

Are you familiar with Chicago? Have you visited the city before? Maybe lived there for a few years? Or, like me, maybe it's where you currently reside. Maybe you grew up in Chicago, but at some point decided you wanted to leave one of America's largest cities for something a little smaller and/or rural.

No matter how familiar you are with Chicago, there's an unfortunate reality you must be aware of: some neighborhoods in Chicago (proper) are worse than others. Far worse. I include "proper" because the geographical area within a city's "city limits" is what is referred to as *proper*. In other words, there are many people who grew up in surrounding areas or suburbs *around* Chicago that will still say they "grew up in Chicago." I'm not saying that to discredit anybody's Chicago allegiance, as this form of communication is similar for a lot of cities. Someone from Lenexa, Kansas might say they're from Kansas City—someone from Royal Oak, Michigan might say they're from Detroit, and so forth.

To be clear, I'm from one of those suburbs right on the outskirts of southside Chicago. For better or worse, that's where I made my grand entrance into this world. And when the hospital dust settled, I found myself in Oak Lawn. And if I had to describe, in a phrase, my experience growing up in Oak Lawn? Classic suburbia.

It was a humble community with nice neighbors; my sister and I felt very fortunate to grow up in that childhood home with two loving parents.

My father, Jack Harnedy, was a wonderful leader both in our home and the community. He worked multiple jobs to support our family, serving as a math teacher, computer teacher, administrator in the Chicago Public School system, and football coach at a local Chicago Catholic high school. (More on the latter shortly). In addition to his teaching and coaching career, Dad picked up a few odd jobs for additional revenue growth for our family. Most prominently, he had a t-shirt business on the side and would make and sell all kinds of shirts for people and their businesses. It was him and his business partner, Ron Szczesniak, who also coached football with my dad for years. I'll never forget the sounds of that press at "Windy City Silkscreening" and the smell of newly printed t-shirts as they dried near that old industrial heater. Dad's hard work was something, in itself, that I looked up to as a kid. When he wasn't teaching or coaching, he was working on another business idea or helping someone with theirs. But there is something *much deeper* than hard work that Jack Harnedy exemplified for our family and community.

It's difficult to put into words. "Networker" is too trite, and "Connector" isn't quite it either. But my father went about his work and life with one thing at the center:

relationships. And so I guess a better descriptor of his life and legacy is better summarized as "Trustworthy." Because, at the end of the day, the best relationships are ones that possess a deep amount of trust. Dad could cultivate and *sustain* a significant amount of trust alongside others, and he did so in and around our Chicago community in spades.

I am forever grateful for that kind of model in the home. "Hero" doesn't even do it justice, even though many kids talk about their dad as a hero. I wouldn't disagree with that sentiment in regard to Jack Harnedy, but it was the *Why* behind his day-to-day philosophy (that made him a hero in my eyes) that truly set the example for my early life and upbringing, and has lasted until the present day.

Dad was in the driver's seat of our family's 1971 Dodge Dart, and we were along for an incredible ride. My sweet mother, Karen, sat in the passenger seat. And me in the backseat alongside my sister, Carrie. That's the car we grew up in while exploring

Chicago. And that's the family unit of four I was blessed with.

For as much as Dad worked and provided for our family, it meant that my sister and I, naturally, just saw more of our Mom around the house. We are better people because of it. Like Dad, Karen Harnedy exuded joy and humility. She taught us how to be creative through art. As an artist herself, she'd spend hours bringing her own paintings and creations to life. As we walked by, we'd get a glimpse into our mother's mind. She'd lead us through arts and crafts in the summer, and help Carrie and I make our own sock puppets and put on little shows and things like that. We'd accompany her to the Chicago Art Institute during our summers. Those little field trips and the art that hung on the walls didn't mean so much to me then, but looking back I am so grateful for early exposure to some of the world's finest works in one of the world's finest museums.

Mom brought a sense of peace and humility to everything we did, and she always helped us understand that you treat others like you want to be treated no matter what the situation. She was involved with our school as a room Mom and a regular chaperone on our class field trips. One elementary school trip stands out—not because of the place we went to, but because of the bus trip to and from the location.

As a kid, it was important who you sat with and where you sat on the bus. There was one kid that had his struggles, not many friends, and a little socially awkward. Nobody ever sat next to him on the bus. Enter my Mom, as we all boarded the bus for the trip, she walked through the bus passing several seats and sat down next to this student. I could hear the whispers, " What's your mom doing?"

At that moment, I learned how important it is to make everybody feel welcomed and loved, no matter who you are, where you're from, or how "socially awkward". When Karen Harnedy's name is spoken by somebody, know it's synonymous with these keywords: love, care, and respect for *all*. How's that for a role model?

Together, Jack and Karen Harnedy made my sister and I feel rich. And that, to me, is the great challenge and joy of parenthood: cultivating a life that is free of financial doubt and/or thought. In other words, I just don't think it should matter what *any* parent or family has in the bank account. I am living proof that growing up, parents have the opportunity to make a kid feel like the richest kid in the room—something that doesn't have to hinge on money.

My parents made sure we had everything we needed to survive, yes, but more importantly, they were *engaged* in our lives. They came to all our sporting events and school activities and encouraged us to try new things. They fostered an environment of mutual support for one another. We celebrated when any four of us experienced a win, and we lamented anytime one of us experienced a loss. That kind of model of empathy translated into my one-on-one relationship with my sister, Carrie.

To this day, my younger sister (by two years) and I are super close. Carrie was my biggest cheerleader in life—cheering me on at football and soccer games. Carrie could have approached our relationship very differently.

For better or worse, I received a lot of attention because of my athletic ability. Carrie embraced it, attended every game, and was waiting for me after every game with a huge smile on her face. And it made it easy to reciprocate in any way that I could. Carrie's love and support impacted me in more ways than one. Growing up with a sibling is one thing, but when that sibling becomes one built-in best friend . . . you realize that, again, being rich is more about the number of loved ones than any amount zeros in a bank account.

One father. One mother. One sister. One Harnedy family in one trusty Dodge Dart and all roads eventually led to a place that made me who I am today: one high school. It was at Mount Carmel High School, located in Woodlawn, Chicago, that I grew from a boy to a man, which was fitting considering it is a Catholic, private high school for boys. And even though it is a brief 30-minute drive from my native Oak Lawn suburb to Woodlawn . . . the two towns are practically a world apart.

No city in America is perfect. In the last 10
to 20 years, as social media has shrunk our
universe and news cycles turn over every
five minutes, American citizens have been
exposed to the good, bad, and ugly of small
and big towns in America alike.
Unfortunately, some towns get a worse rep
than others—sometimes that rep is
warranted, but other times it's misguided
based on one or two events in America's
history. For instance, people might hear of
Ferguson, Missouri, and think of the racial
rioting and tension in that city in 2015, but
for those events alone to define a city just
isn't fair. There are real families living in
Ferguson, and many of them are great
people making a real difference in the world.
In the same way, there are people who might
live in or around Chicago that hear of the
south side Chicago area of Woodlawn and
think of a rough neighborhood. Well, they
are and aren't correct. The fact of the matter
is, yes, Woodlawn has had its share of
economic hardship, compounded on top of
an ever-growing problem with violence
throughout Chicago's south side. Such sad
occurrences that have happened in a place

that means a lot to me. But economic struggle and brutal violence *do not* tell the full story.

The full story looks a little more like this: life in a community is hard. And when people live close to each other, conflict is sure to arise. Unfortunately, jobs and finances, and familial circumstances can *all* contribute to conflict, and the real issue lies in conflict resolution or lack thereof. When you look at "nicer" neighborhoods throughout America, some of them only seem that way because people are more capable of hiding or running away from conflict. But these are different (and bigger) topics for another day.

The real point is that there are great people who live in and around Woodlawn, and I'm thankful for my time driving to and from that place throughout my upbringing. Why spend so much time there? Because Woodlawn is where one of Chicago's oldest and most well-known high schools is located: Mount Carmel High School.

And for me, it's the place I alluded to earlier in this chapter—the workplace of my father, Jack Harnedy. At Mount Carmel, my father served faithfully as an assistant football coach for +15 years. He was good at what he did, and he loved what he did.

Mount Carmel High School and the Harnedy family have deep roots, and it's hard to explain just how much of an impact that community has had on our family at large. My father was a student there and played football. One of his brothers (my Uncle Kevin) was an accomplished wrestler at Mount Carmel. Another one of his brothers, whom I affectionately know as Uncle Bill, chose to take a bit of a different route with high school and college and was the brave Harnedy boy to break the mold and pursue full-time ministry. My dad's sister, Maureen, didn't really have a choice in the matter, seeing as Mount Carmel is an all-boys school — so she attended another school nearby our hometown. But the Harnedy + Mount Carmel connection was really cemented around two people. But before I get to those people . . .

Just a quick word on one's local high school community and the reason it's important for me to set the Mount Carmel stage for you in this book. You see, I had a special relationship with this school located on the south side of Chicago. But your high school memories, experiences, and recollections are obviously going to be different. Whenever I bring up Mount Carmel, know that it's not some roundabout way of me trying to "relive the glory days" but more so paying homage to the past *so that* I can capitalize on my future. If you are lucky enough to have had a positive high school experience as I did, that's great! I hope that you do recognize how that time shaped and molded you into the person you are today. If you had a *negative* high school experience, then yes . . . it's appropriate to move on accordingly. But I think that "moving on" can *also* mean gleaning from your negative experience and living your life in such a way that creates a better environment or greater set of opportunities for young people you might come into contact with. In other words, how might you live in such a way that gives teenagers the opportunity you never had?

Alright, so a final word on dad before moving to the real mountain mover at Mount Carmel. As in the "two people" previously mentioned that contributed so many years to that school and impacted thousands of young men's lives as a result.

For me, growing up with a present and encouraging dad is one thing. But to watch him pour so much of his time, wisdom, and love into others was just a huge bonus. I mentioned Jack Harnedy was a math, and computer teacher, and administrator for Chicago Public Schools, but the football field at Mount Carmel is where I got to watch him take young boys and guide them into promising young men. I just looked up to him so much for that, and it showed me that life isn't so much about *where* you're planted or *what* you've been called to—no, Jack Harnedy taught me it's *how* you're stewarding the *where* and *what*.

As for the "where," my family grew up on the south side of Chicago. Neither the suburbs nor the urban area was or is perfect by any stretch, but that is where we called home. The "what" contained day-to-day ongoings for my mother and father to keep a roof over our head and my sister and I thriving within our little unit of four. We had so much growing up—all those years supporting one another in our endeavors, and fond memories of that little Dodge Dart cruising around town. My dad stewarded his duties well as a husband and father, and his presence then affects the way I live my life now. It's a blessing that so many men across the country can say the same—all because he was just as faithful during his day job as he was at home.

So where did *he* get it from? Who were the people my dad looked up to in *his* life that allowed him to conduct himself in such a way? Well, remember that phrase "mountain mover" I slid in a few paragraphs ago? I chose those two words carefully. Walking around a private high school for boys can sometimes feel like there are these little mountains walking around—strapping young men who are top athletes in the area, focused on football, basketball, baseball, and otherwise. But of course, they aren't *actual* mountains. Many of them wouldn't hit peak height until maybe their early college years. No, what *really* makes these young individuals seem like mountains is something nearly every teenage boy has to confront whether he realizes it or not: ego.

Perhaps no greater time in a young kid's life does he or she experience "entitlement" quite like junior or senior year of high school. And why shouldn't they? We've all been there. You've got your driver's license for the first time. You might be a "big man on campus" or just feel good about life in general because you have more freedom. College and real life are on the horizon, which is exciting but you aren't *quite there* yet and don't have to pay the bills at home, etc. Yep, high school presents its own set of challenges—one day you're feeling low in a valley, and the next day you're standing high on a mountaintop.

In both circumstances, it helps to have a guide to keep you in line. Someone to help you up when you're feeling down, or to help you down when you're feeling up. And although my dad fulfilled his role in this manner, it was the person above him that embodied what made Mount Carmel's culture and mission so special—my dad's mother. A person is largely responsible for our family's presence on the south side of

Chicago. A person who served this all-boys school so faithfully for 36 years—20 more than my dad would end up working. A person who set the tone for our family as a whole, as she woke up each day with a purpose and vigor for life that was truly infectious. The wonderful mountain mover of Mount Carmel. My grandmother, Betty Harnedy.

3

Betty Prosser was 19 years old when she married 23-year-old William 'Red' Harnedy. They grew up in Chicago and lived a few minutes away from each other, but didn't meet until high school when Betty met William on the corner of a drug store hanging out with kids in the neighborhood. But after cultivating a basic friendship, something happened that would take 'Red' far away from that corner.

Like many young men after the events at Pearl Harbor, 'Red' enlisted in the Marines in December of 1941. He was deployed to the Pacific almost immediately and went on to serve our country faithfully. It was a role he held through 1944 when he visited Chicago during his time on leave. That trip back to Chicago is when he and Betty got married.

Two young kids who were "too young" by today's standards, but who would go on to live 56 years together in marriage, birth four children, and impact thousands of lives in the process.

After getting married, the two moved to California where 'Red' would await his next assignment. When the assignment came, it was shortly after 'Red' and Betty found out Betty was pregnant with her first child: my Uncle Bill.

What happened next is somewhat of a legend in the Harnedy family, but it's a true story—a moment where Betty marched into the Commanding Officer's office and advocated for her husband to not be sent to the Pacific after finding out about being with child.

Well, what we don't know, to this day, were her words exactly to negotiate his terms of service, but whatever she said . . . it worked. My grandfather was held back from the Pacific and re-stationed as an MP in San Diego. That's where he finished out his career in the Marines, and when the war ended in 1945, he and Betty had a decision to make.

All signs pointed to their hometown of Chicago, where 'Red' would go home to help his father run their family's milk-delivery service. They had three more children, my aunt Maureen, my father Jack, and my uncle Kevin while working as a hostess at The Martinique Drury Lane Theater in Evergreen Park, Illinois—located on the south side of Chicago.

For Betty, she helped The Martinique, then in its early days, establish itself as a premier theater and entertainment center. She was a model for hard work and grace while serving as a loving mother to my father and his siblings.

While working at The Martinique, she met hundreds of unique people, as you could imagine—an entertainment center outside of a diverse community. She learned so much there in the early days of her career, I'm sure, about something that can't really be taught: cultivating meaningful relationships and interactions with people. In today's age, so much is automated for us and/or performed from behind a screen. But Betty was faithful in her very real, very interpersonal position at The Martinique, and it made her an incredibly *dynamic presence* whenever you were in the same room with her. As a hostess, she was more of a guide and people looked to her for direction. Among the many connections she made while working there, a number of individuals had connections to a local boys' private high school: Mount Carmel in Woodlawn.

Before I get to the opportunity that would change the course of her life and career, it's worth noting what Betty's husband was doing those first years in Chicago—getting a milk delivery company up and running. From cow to farmer, farmer to manufacturer, manufacturer to 'Red', 'Red' to your doorstep. Seems like a simple formula, but I can't imagine the hundreds of decisions that my grandfather had to make in those early days to pursue his dream and provide for his family at the same time. It's easy to look back now and think that he simply owned and operated his own milk service company, but I know the truth is a lot more complex than that. Yet what we deem as complex was merely his reality: up at 3 a.m. each morning, willing to work to make his dream come true —and place milk bottles on someone's doorstep.

Hosting an event. Delivering milk. Two best friends living in Chicago with a dream to expand their family and "put down roots" in an exciting and growing city. In many ways, Betty and Red's story is what many view as "the American dream" but behind every real American dream (or at least that one that succeeds) is a person who is willing to put in the work to make it happen, and lead with faith in the process.

All of that faith and hard work eventually led my grandmother to an opportunity that would alter her career, and affect thousands of people in the years that followed.

It was the principal of Mount Carmel who approached my grandmother about a job opportunity. The role was Administrative Assistant and, apparently, he thought her hostess capabilities at The Martinique would translate well to a private high school setting. Thank God he had that hunch as the Martinique stopped buying milk from my grandfather around the same time to go with a "cheaper" supplier and my grandfather was insistent that Betty move on. That hunch couldn't have been more correct.

She started in the role as a part-time Administrative Assistant but quickly fell in love with the people on staff and of course the students themselves. She eventually transitioned into a full-time role at the school and went on to serve Mount Carmel for 36 years—while undertaking responsibilities throughout various jobs and opportunities at the school. But, for the most part, she stayed in her lane and made sure everyone else stayed in theirs. And lest you think she ruled with an iron fist, that's not quite it. Betty Harnedy carried herself with *purpose* each day she stepped inside that school, and everyone knew it. Out of that purpose, it challenged onlookers to do the same. It didn't matter if it was the principal, the janitor, or Donovan McNabb. Everybody respected Betty Harnedy because of the way she loved and respected others. She gave her best each day on the job and expected the best from any and all at Mount Carmel — simply because she *knew* everyone at the school was absolutely capable of giving their best each day. And yes, I did just say NFL quarterback and legend Donovan McNabb. He graduated from Mount Carmel in 1994 and would go on to dominate the NCAA and NFL playing fields throughout the 1990s and 2000s. But the one person who never backed down from Donovan was my sweet grandmother — standing at a towering 5'4". She asked the best of him, with no special treatment, because she asked the best of everyone in school, and knew we were all capable of MVP status.

Which leads to me. I did *not* have the same kind of NFL trajectory as Donovan McNabb, but I myself was a different kind of grateful because Betty Harnedy was so much more to me than an Administrative Assistant at Mount Carmel High School. She was my grandmother. And you know what else? She was my carpool ride each morning.

At 7:10 am. That's the time seared into my memory, and it's the time that carries so much significance for me to this day. Sometimes I'll be at work, notice "7:10" on the clock and *almost* feel the urge that she's pulling up to my curb again to pick me up for school. Kind of funny how time works, isn't it?

Betty made it very plain to me: if I was not standing on the curb each morning at 7:10 am ready for school, I would have to find another way to Mount Carmel.

Sounds harsh? Maybe to an average high school kid who just wanted to sleep in for a few extra minutes each morning. But I knew the heart behind Betty's methodology: she had a job to do, and I wasn't going to deter her from being the best worker she knew how to be. In addition, she knew I was *more than capable* of meeting her each morning at 7:10 am. Together, we knew that if her husband could get up each morning at

3 am to rev up milk delivery, she and I could be off toward Mount Carmel by 7:10 sharp.

Betty and 'Red' lived about two miles from my parents' home. We were right on the way during her drive to Mount Carmel—a drive she had done for years before I finally got to high school. And each morning, like clockwork, she'd pull up to the curb, and I'd get into her car and greet her. But I was rarely alone. Two others joined us during those morning drives—a neighbor of mine and another boy who lived around the corner from our block in Oak Lawn. The drive was about 20-30 minutes to Mount Carmel, all depending on traffic and how feisty Betty was feeling on the road that morning. Yet we boys cherished each moment of wisdom we could glean from her in that timeframe, even if we didn't *fully* understand at the moment. We talked about everything from athletics at Mount Carmel to the weather to her growing up in the city to you name it. She had incredible stories and was a true joy to be around. Us three boys felt privileged to spend a little extra time with this woman before she became

"Mrs. Harnedy" after parking and walking into school together.

When we didn't converse in the car, smooth jazz typically filled the airwaves — appropriately filling the car's silence with soothing morning music that calmed each of us before the day ahead.

There were days, however, when the silence looked a little different. The silence that came on Mondays often followed a Mount Carmel football victory from the previous Friday night. Betty would pull up to the curb just a *few* minutes early—around 7:05 am— and take us to the legendary Wolf's Bakery in Evergreen Park for celebratory donuts. The rest of the drive was filled with an excited silence as we stuffed our faces with dough and icing.

Those mornings also presented an opportunity to watch Betty in her element. After parking in the lot, my friends would walk into the school and go to class. I'd follow Betty as she delivered donuts to the football coaching staff. As a young freshman, I was pretty intimidated by that place! But not Betty. She walked right into that room as if she was one of the coaches herself, set down the donuts, congratulated the coaches on their victory, and walked back out into the halls—prepared to fulfill another day's work at Mount Carmel.

Now, a quick note on that coach's office. Throughout elementary and middle school, I had visited the office many times—as my dad was a tenured football coach at Mount Carmel. But my father's last year coaching high school football was after my Freshman year. I went all of my high school career with my dad as . . . my dad . . . and my coach for at least one year. And I found that to be an incredible experience to bond over the game and my time as a player even if he also focused on 70 other high school boys my age.

My dad was still involved at the school, so it was fun to still have him around while I was a student. But I didn't feel his presence quite like Betty's. She was just, naturally, more present in the hallways—walking to and from classroom to classroom as she helped keep the school humming. It really was such a great transition for her from The Martinique to Mount Carmel. But she was *so much more* than a hostess in either place. She was a calming and steady presence. If she was ever sick and had to miss school, you felt her aura gone from the hallways, and something just felt off. All the students knew it, and it was the same from generation to generation that walked those grounds.

Because of her status at Mount Carmel, I felt honored each morning I got to spend with her on the way to school. And when we weren't eating donuts, and when smooth jazz wasn't filling the air, we would talk about anything and *everything*.

A lot of conversation took place surrounding the school itself. She knew the teachers and classrooms inside and out and gave me great advice on how to carry myself in the classroom. She had a deep fascination with people, and it showed in her craft: keeping the trains moving. She knew the strengths and weaknesses of everyone on staff at Mount Carmel, and it made our school a well-functioning institution for as long as she was tenured. To say Mount Carmel was left a better place than when she found it would be a total understatement. And I can confidently say the same about her and me during those early morning rides to school.

It makes me think of interpersonal skills or soft skills and how some people say those are things that just can't be taught. But the truth is, those things *can* be taught—it just doesn't look like the same kind of teaching as teaching a kid to do math or operate a science experiment. Those things are important as well, but in the information age, my grandmother's example of curiosity, discipline, and time well spent is a message for the day.

The only thing better than free donuts on a victory Monday morning was the free advice she dealt, and I'm grateful for that to this day.

But here's maybe the most important lesson, and I believe will set up the rest of this book quite nicely: Betty knew full well that the most important person in the room (or car) was the person right across from you. It didn't matter who you were, where you came from, what your title was, or what that person could do for you . . . she was simply invested in people because they were human and had a soul worth caring for. I can't think of a better attitude and disposition to be leading future generations in the high school setting like she did. And so to know that each morning I got *her* undivided attention for a few minutes before each school is humbling to think about.

In conversation, everything around her stopped. She'd look you in the eye, and you felt the care and warmth about her. But she was focused and intent. Her eyes didn't glaze over. She wanted to know about *you* and people walked away from those interactions feeling both refreshed and more confident because she *saw* you.

The fundamental longing of every human being is to be recognized, and Betty made sure of that everywhere she went.

From Chicago to California and back to Chicago, Betty and 'Red' Harnedy didn't exactly know what the ensuing decades would bring, but on the other side of that move, I can confidently say that thousands of people affected by their move is one of the results. Can you imagine that? Day-to-day, early morning faithfulness at one's job impacted thousands (maybe millions!) of lives because of their discipline and intentionality. You don't wake up at 3 am to deliver milk if you don't care about the health and well-being of humans and the local community. And you don't devote that much time, energy, and effort to a school for 30+ years if you don't truly care about making the world a better place.

Although so much of society is focused on "changing the world" by way of some big business idea or getting famous, I'm here to tell you that changing the world can be as simple as showing up and doing your job to the best of your ability. That's what Betty did. And I had a front-row passenger seat for the whole thing. I'm just a kid who got lucky and didn't just watch her serve at school but also watched her treat everyone in front of her like the most important person that they were.

If you and I ever interact in person, I can only hope you notice something similar about me. And I hope that you glean wisdom from the advice she told me and put on display:

That the good work of a humble hostess is to see everyone in the room and make sure they get to their ultimate destination.

Thank you, Betty, for making sure we got to ours.

4
_____

There's something unique about the long-snapper position in football: the most important person is the one right across from you. See, even Betty knew a thing or two about football. But the reason this fact is "unique" about the long-snapper position is that the person across from you is actually standing about 30-40 yards away, downfield.

After you snap the ball back and between your legs, the punter (who is arguably tied for first as the "most important person" on a punt play) receives the ball and winds up his leg to boot it downfield. In that short time span, your job as a long-snapper is to sprint downfield and cause some chaos. There is more to be said on the art of the punt play, but those few seconds from the time a punter punts a ball and the punt returner *receives* a ball are some of the most exhilarating seconds in a football game.

Anything can happen. Guys are trying to throw you, the long-snapper, off course. But the idea and thought of tackling the ball carrier is so exciting—there is a good amount of adrenaline, and it's a play that not many think about in football but actually encapsulates so much about what makes the game great.

Football is fleeting. The game goes by quickly, and between the opening kick-off and final whistle, there is a lot of chaos. There are highs and lows in the middle of those events, but one thing is certain: when the final whistle *does* blow, you possess a much closer brotherhood to the guys you just went to battle with.

It's having a common goal. It's putting in the hours of work beforehand. And it's the acceptance of victory OR loss as an outcome, and knowing that, if you're lucky, you get to reenact the whole process again the following week.

Every week that I had in high school to play alongside those young men—my friends—was an honor. Talk about the "most important person is the one in front of you." Betty understood that as true in regard to her family, friends, and colleagues, and it produced a special kind of trickle-down effect throughout the rest of the school—our football team included. We cared for one another on a human level, and it translated into our team chemistry on a week-to-week basis.

Yet while the most important *opposing* player for a long-snapper is downfield, there is someone even more important on your own team: the person next to you. As any football player knows, for success to occur you need 11 guys doing their job—if it's only 10, you will lose. And for that varsity team at Mount Carmel High School, the person next to me was Kevin Dowling.

When we think of our best friends from childhood, we sometimes think of our *very first friends* from elementary school or playdates with our parent's friends and their kids. But high school is a different story for multiple reasons. You're that much more grown and developed, you devote more time and energy to organized sports or activities, and you experience a different level of freedom in a number of ways . . . like behind the wheel of a car for the first time. All those reasons were true for me, but my personal relationships were intensified at Mount Carmel because it was a completely new school to me.

Mount Carmel, as a private high school for boys, was like a melting pot for academically advanced and/or athletically inclined individuals in the Chicago land area. We had all sorts of young boys at that school from all walks of life, but the fun and prestige that came from attending a well-known school in the area made us feel less like boys and more like young men on the brink of the rest of our lives.

When the excitement drifted into entitlement, we had a great set of staff, coaches, and elders like Betty Harnedy to keep us in line and make sure that we never took an opportunity at education from Mount Carmel for granted.

I was grateful for humble leadership from the top down at Mount Carmel, but I was even more thankful for friendship from some incredible peers who exhibited the same.

To say the competitive spirit was alive in both education and sports at Mount Carmel is an understatement. It was up to individual students to make the sacrifices and commitments necessary to achieve a high level of success.

During the football offseason, I made the decision to work on my strength and endurance with a personal trainer, John Clark, as well as my team. Working out with John required waking up at 4 am, driving to downtown Chicago and completing my first workout of the day by 6 am (a ritual that continues to this day, 25+ years later). What I didn't know is that working out with John at his gym would open up an opportunity that would foreshadow my career as an adult.

Chicago Mayor Richard M. Daley also worked out with a trainer at the same small gym as I did—at the same time each morning! Little did I know that he and his wife had an established relationship with my grandmother, Betty. He and I spoke often in the mornings, and we built our own relationship with each other. Like many high schoolers at the time, I took French classes. I learned that the President of France at the time, Jacques Chirac was coming to Chicago to visit Mayor Daley and schools across the city. Thinking it would be a long shot, I asked Mayor Daley if our French class could come to one of the events and meet Jacques Chirac.

In my mind, I thought I could leverage this move for extra credit in class. Mayor Daley enthusiastically agreed. That evening, the secret service called my parents and exchanged information—we were confirmed to attend an event later in the week. I went to school the next day and tested my French teacher.

I asked a simple question: "Hey, I heard Jacques Chirac is in town this week. If we meet him, could the entire French class receive an A for the remainder of the year?"

The French teacher laughed and brushed it off as a silly high schooler asking a ridiculous question. He said, "Of course, you would all get A's the rest of the year."

Later that day, the secret service called Mount Carmel High School and confirmed with the principal and my French teacher that we would attend an event with Mayor Daley and Jacques Chirac. Not only did we attend the event and have a wonderful time . . . and we also ALL got A's the rest of the year. My teacher kept his word!

This was my first "sale" on a large scale, and I believe this was the moment, ingrained in the back of my mind, that I could do sales for a long-term career if football didn't pan out.

Many of the friends I met at Mount Carmel *had* attended grammar school together in the area—therefore, I felt a little behind the eight-ball at first. Even though I had a couple of ties to high school through my dad and grandmother, it didn't make this small fish in a giant pond seem any easier. But a few friends really "welcomed me into the fold" so to speak—especially in the first few weeks and months of that first fall of 1992. You just can't underestimate the impact a high school kid can have on another person, and that first group of friends—largely derived from our time on the freshman football team—became some of my closest friends in the years that followed.

Among that group was Kevin. He was one of those kids from grammar school, who came to Mount Carmel with an established group of friends. Kevin made me feel like we'd been friends forever.

Now, we also had another connecting force between us: Kevin and I both played on the offensive line for our Mount Carmel freshman football team. And thus began a friendship forged in fire (if you will)—anyone who has played on the offensive line knows that the offensive line is where football games are lost or won.

Yes, the quarterback is the most important position on the field. And yes, I don't disagree with "defense wins championships" but the offensive line is in charge of 1) *protecting* the most important position on the field and 2) stopping the *opponent's* defense is coming at full force.

The offensive line does not get a lot of glory. Their names are hardly announced over the loudspeaker. A right guard, for example, will rarely receive the game ball or MVP trophy. And a lineman's name won't show up in the newspaper the next day. But that's also part of what makes linemen close as a unit . . . they won't get much love from the outside world, so they need to take care of one another and lift each other up on a consistent basis.

Enter Kevin Dowling. He epitomized everything an offensive lineman is and should be known for: humility, selflessness, tenacity, sportsmanship, and grit. His attitude on the field gave way to a caring, bright, and inclusive demeanor off the field —from which I benefitted alongside many other classmates at Mount Carmel.

What started on the freshman squad carried over into our sophomore year, and eventually our junior and senior seasons on the varsity team. Playing a few years alongside a good friend creates a kind of camaraderie that is hard to break apart. Kevin typically played guard—the interior offensive line—whereas I played to his left or right as an offensive tackle. He did his job. I did mine. We knew that each other's footwork and timing affected running and pass plays, and we took pride as leaders of the offensive line. Not *the* leaders, but two leaders on an offensive unit of 11 working toward a common goal: a state title.

Our class formed a pretty tight bond on the football field at Mount Carmel, but I, unfortunately, didn't see Kevin too much during school. In short, Kevin had to put in extra work in the classroom because of a couple of learning setbacks he had to endure growing up, which put him a little behind once we got to high school. But you know what? He *never* complained or worried about the extra effort he had to put in to keep up with his grades and workload. In fact, it actually motivated guys on the team to see how hard he worked on *and* off the field— myself included.

The same mentality went for his friendships. He cared for those in his path, and not just the cool or popular kids that every high school in America contains. Kevin looked out for the outsiders and those on the fringe because he didn't want *them* to experience any kind of setback in school, football, or life. I was "Exhibit A" as he knew I didn't attend grammar school with his group of friends growing up, but he made me feel seen, heard, and respected when I got to Mount Carmel. What else does a freshman in high school need or want?

The Dowlings had a great basement, and our group of friends in high school spent a lot of time down there. It's another funny thing about high school: a lot of "hanging out" usually occurs at the greatest basements in town. Not to knock on houses without a cool basement, it just seems a natural phenomenon: kids love bean bags, video games, big TVs, and a little bit of privacy. Or at least that's what we loved—your experience might've been a little different.

Another thing high schoolers loved in the early nineties? Talking on the phone. I know

. . . either you're reading this with a bit of nostalgia, or wondering why kids would ever talk on the phone to each other in high school. If the latter, just know that phones used to have cords. And Snapchat wouldn't come on the scene for another couple of decades.

Kevin and I were kind of like Josh and Billy from the Tom Hanks film, *Big*—two best friends who talked each night away in their youth. We spent so many nights just catching up about our school days or about the football team and who we were going to play against the next weekend. Although I don't recall many of the specifics surrounding those conversations, it's more so the fact I had *someone like him* to pick up the phone and carry on a call just like a best friend should.

Yet there *is* a specific memory that speaks to the kind of person Kevin was, and the kind of "forged through fire" our relationship endured.

It was during our junior year at Mount Carmel, and we had just played our first playoff game of the year. The game was against Buffalo Grove, and we pulverized them. I'm sure there were some great kids on that Buffalo Grove team, but we were on a mission that year, and it felt like all the hard work we had put in as freshmen and sophomores were really paying off in a cool way. We won that first playoff game and took some time to celebrate before preparing for the following week.

Two things were certain as we prepared to celebrate: Betty would be bringing donuts to the coaching staff on Monday, but first . . . Kevin and I would be eating giant burritos right after showering and getting dressed.

Remember that freedom you experience behind the wheel for the first time in high school? It is a very real and very powerful thing—worth mentioning the great Uncle Ben quote from *Spiderman*: "With great power comes great responsibility."

For some reason, Kevin and I formed a little tradition to yield that power for post-game burritos. It started that junior year, and we turned it into a ritual after Mount Carmel victories. After all, we were growing boys that happened to be six feet tall and up, and pushing 300lbs. It's safe to say one burrito alone wasn't going to cut it.

Burrito Station. That wasn't the name of the tradition, but the actual place we'd get post-game burritos in high school. Super burritos from Burrito Station on a Saturday night. Looking back, that's a fitting way to put it — our high school football games took place on a Saturday night, unlike many schools across the country that play on Friday nights. It's just how our school system worked. So when I rolled to the game in my dad's Ford Explorer, we all knew the plan was to take care of business during the game, hop back in the Explorer, and demolish super burritos after the game.

It was 1994 and not only did we defeat Buffalo Grove for our first playoff win, but me, Kevin, and a couple of other teammates planned on taking down multiple burritos at Burrito Station afterward . . . per tradition. Most of that time happened according to plan, but after we piled into my dad's Explorer (heading to Burrito Station), we didn't know our lives were about to change.

Hopping on the highway and driving for a few miles before exiting, it was a pretty simple drive to get there. Yet there's something to recall from earlier in the chapter . . . that sometimes, as a high school student who is just enjoying life with his buddies, there is a subtle pride and/or entitlement that can creep in—like nothing can touch you. It's funny how a high school football victory and Burrito Station can make you feel, subconsciously, on top of the world. That "on top of the world" feeling came crashing down when I turned the corner after the exit ramp, hydroplaned over a set of train tracks, (from heavy rain the night before), and rammed my dad's Explorer into a telephone pole.

Kevin was in the passenger seat. He wasn't wearing his seatbelt. The force from the impact threw him forward, and the rest was a blur. I don't remember the exact moment of impact, but when I gathered myself seconds after, I immediately checked on Kevin.

All the excitement we had just experienced. All the years of friendship and phone calls and super burritos came to mind, and ultimate relief took the place of those thoughts when Kevin responded to my voice. But he didn't just respond.

"Wow, that was close," Kevin said. He told me his head simply hit the front panel in front of the glass—we both knew it could've been much worse had the impact catapulted him through the windshield.

"I'm so sorry, Jack," he continued, "I should've been wearing my seatbelt."

. . . Kevin Dowling apologized after my error behind the wheel. Did I have control over the car as it was hydroplaning? No. But maybe I could've driven slower. And yes, he should have been wearing his seatbelt, but it was nobody's real fault—just a car accident that happened and shocked any sort of entitlement we had that night back to reality. We *weren't* invincible like we maybe thought we were . . . like *any* high school kid might think at times. It's something we talked about later that night on the phone.

The car was definitely totaled. Although it was an accident, I knew I'd have to own it when I called my dad and told him. He got in his car to come to pick us up. I was just glad nobody got seriously hurt, and I knew it would be my dad's overarching feeling as well. When he got to us he joked, "Glad you moved the D-Line better than you did this telephone poll." A few of the guys went on to Burrito Station afterward, but I went home with my dad. Kevin and I hopped on a call a little bit later to process what had just happened. We talked for a couple of hours about everything—the game, the burritos, but mostly the car accident. I double-checked, again and again, to ensure he was OK. He was. Yet maybe the most important thing we discussed was how we weren't going to take life for granted from there on out. Although I already saw Kevin as someone who squeezed every bit out of life in the way he loved others and lifted them up, I could tell the future would never really be the same for both of us.

We didn't go on to win a state championship that year, which was our original goal. But after the season was through, it made us hungrier for what would come next. And I'm not just talking about burritos. Our new goal was to go out on top as seniors. It was the first thing Kevin and the rest of our teammates discussed when the playoffs ended in a loss: how next year was our year.

We worked out that winter, spring, and summer like maniacs. We ate . . . a lot. And kept growing as humans and student-athletes. Around that time is when I started to get some interest from college football programs (more on that a little later) but any formal college decision would have to wait as our Mount Carmel team had unfinished business.

Where some of that aforementioned entitlement reaches its peak for some kids during their senior year, a few of us had a humbling experience in the form of a car accident months before to keep us grounded. We didn't take a day for granted going into our senior year, and made sure to lift others up and encourage them with that same kind of attitude—an attitude that says "don't take today for granted; give this life everything you have."

Something along those lines is the attitude we had during the summer of 1995 entering workouts and pre-season practices. A very hot Chicago July gave way to an unprecedented August heat—a summer where more than 500 people passed away due to the extreme heat. Three-a-days were the norm in high school football at the time, but the heat made it seem like we were out there way longer than just a one or two-hour practice. Did the pads help? Not quite. But we were hungry for a common goal—to win a state championship—and knew our attitude in August would reflect our actions later that fall.

On August 11th, we were in the middle of one of those two-a-day practices. And much like the hydroplane experience, to nobody's fault but an extreme accident, Kevin Dowling collapsed on our football practice field.

We were just running through practice like normal when I noticed coaches running over to a player on the field, and it didn't take me long to recognize it was Kevin.

"I'm so sorry, Jack."

Those words I recalled from the passenger seat. Kevin apologized to *me* for something that wasn't his fault.

"Not your fault, Kevin. I just hydroplaned. I'm glad you're OK."

What I would have given to tell him the same on the field that day. That "You're gonna be OK, Kev" but I didn't have time. The coaches were already carrying him off the field in a rush for the school pool to cool him off. Kevin had had a heatstroke in the middle of the blazing hot Chicago heat, and every minute afterward mattered. Every coach did what they could to save our friend's life—just a kid with the whole rest of his life ahead of him. With each second, our team of teenagers knew the increasing seriousness of the situation. But at the same time, it's like each of us was paralyzed—one of those moments when reality hit us yet again: we were just kids playing a game we loved. None of us were ready for what would come next.

Kevin was rushed in an ambulance to UChicago Medicine. He underwent an emergency liver and kidney transplant.

Kevin was alive. He wasn't fully recovered by any means, but he was stable. All was seemingly going well and improving for Kevin until the morning of our first game that senior year. We were to play Joliet Catholic to kick off our football season. I'll never forget my dad telling me Kevin had gone into cardiac arrest—his new liver apparently experienced sudden failure while he was shaving with his dad that morning in the hospital.

Days prior, Kevin had told me he would be suited up in his letterman's jacket with us on the field against Joliet Catholic. I tried to joke with him "Yeah, right!" because I knew he still had a really long road to recovery. I was just grateful he had survived his heatstroke and in an instant . . . he was gone.

His goal was to be with us on the field that Saturday evening and each of us knew he was—it just wasn't in a letterman's jacket. His spirit was with us that night as we absolutely clobbered Joliet Catholic. They didn't stand a chance. We had so much adrenaline and were playing for something so much bigger than football. To be honest,

I'm not sure how we were able to go out and function that night on the field, but it was one of those moments where we just persisted through because we *knew* it was what Kevin would've wanted us to do. And so we did. And I drove to Burrito Station afterward.

And then I went home. And sat in the driver's seat of my dad's (repaired) Ford Explorer. And I wept for one of the first and best friends I ever had. I still struggle with Kevin's sudden death to this very day—the recollection of which, decades after the fact, still brings out raw and indescribable emotion. Even the sound of bagpipes (that played at his funeral) or a simple mention of Kevin to my wife or kids brings me right back to the summer of 1995. As hard as those moments are, they fuel my passion for living "like Kevin" every day.

5

O n the cover of this book, there's a
whistle. I haven't talked about it
much until this moment, but I was saving its
importance for after Kevin's life, story, and
death—something that happened *far too soon*
and something that no parent should have to
endure. Mr. Dowling was simply doing
something all fathers do at one point in time
with their sons— shave for a clean-feeling
face—yet he didn't know it would be the last
time they'd spend together.

One moment he was on the road to recovery
from a heatstroke under the blazing Chicago
sun, and the next moment we were playing
the first game of our senior season in

memoriam of our friend—*my* best friend I had had until that moment. I don't know if Kevin and I would have remained friends throughout college and life thereafter, but I certainly like to think so—he was the kind of loyal person that prioritized relationships over everything else: school, football, and yes . . . even burritos.

Because it was never about the actual Burrito Station tradition we created for after Saturday night football games . . . It was always about a little extra time with a friend who made me feel a little extra cared for during my teenage years. For that reason, I am forever grateful for the life and legacy that Kevin left behind. You might think that it was just my life he had such a profound impact on, but you'd be wrong—*thousands* of lives and families were impacted by his premature death, and it's my hope, in telling his story in this book, that thousands more would look to his example and realize one thing: Kevin Dowling played until the final whistle, and you need to as well.

After Kevin's death, it took a few days for reality to set in—this was obviously the case as we were somehow able to go out and play a football game the same night we learned about his death. As a bunch of teenage kids, we simply channeled the anger and sadness, and the rest of our emotions into the game itself because we truly believed it was what Kevin would have wanted.

The game happened. We obliterated the other team in honor of Kevin. And then I cried for my friend. The following week at school was where things started to set in — our friend was gone, and many of us had to confront the death of a loved one (and peer) for the first time.

We mourned as a team and as a community. We went to his funeral, and it was the saddest day of my life. At the same time, we celebrated the life Kevin lived and the lives he was able to impact during his time on earth. It was around that time I started to think about how I might honor his life for the rest of mine.

What would Kevin do in this situation? How would he attack a certain problem or persist through adversity? Who in the room would Kevin gravitate toward? And how would he make *them* feel like the most important person in the room?

Our football coach, Frank Lenti, challenged us throughout the rest of the season—he'd say, "Let's not dwell on how Kevin died, but how Kevin lived." That quote shaped and molded the remainder of our senior year, and we reminded each other of it often. Although the adrenaline carried us through that game right after he died, we really needed to find the courage to continue on with the rest of the season—to play our best for Kevin, and try not to break down at the same time. It was a difficult senior season, and even though we didn't accomplish our goal of a state championship title (lost in the State Championship title game) we all knew we were playing for something much bigger than a trophy that year.

The fact that Kevin Dowling—a 17-year-old son, friend, and football player—could impact the life of a guy in his mid-forties (me) is pretty wild, but it's the truth. And I know I'm not the only one. There are countless other lives Kevin impacts each day, and I hope you are now among them.

Kevin played until the final whistle, and I hope you do too. His whistle came way too early, but it's, unfortunately, the way life works—we're here today and never know if it might be our last. So how will you live accordingly? Something to consider tomorrow . . . after your alarm wakes you up, and you roll out of bed, snap, and go. Remind yourself that Kevin gave everything he had once the ball was snapped.

Eventually, the final whistle blew on our senior season, and we had to confront another hard reality: high school was coming to a close, and life was just around the corner.

Of course, many of us had already thought about the next steps in terms of college decisions and where we all might go outside of Mount Carmel. It was a sobering thought, but one that every high school student confronts, and it means you're "leaving the nest" so to speak, whether you're going to college or getting your first job.

For me, I knew it was an opportunity to take my love for football and the talent I had cultivated to the next level.

So much of my high school playing career centered around that team of boys becoming men, and then Kevin's untimely death that forced us to grow up real fast. Probably *too fast* but it's the way it was. Another element of growing up *was* thinking about the next steps after high school, and I made up my mind sometime around my sophomore or junior year that I wanted to play football at the next level.

Therefore, I made plans for and eventually attended college football camps (mostly during the summertime) at the universities of Michigan, Wisconsin, and Minnesota. Somewhere *around* Chicago is where I was thinking for school, and I *did* want to play at the highest level I could possibly play at, so the thought of playing at a school in the Big 10 conference sounded awesome to me. All of those campuses are wonderful, and attending those camps allowed me to meet each respective coaching staff. One thing that helped me stick out at those camps? My size. It might go without saying, but you can't really step onto a Big 10 football field (at least as an offensive lineman) if your frame isn't hovering around 6'7" " and 300 lbs. Well, I had enough super burritos in me by junior year to meet those specifications, and it showed.

And make no mistake, my goal *was* to play on the offensive line at one of these schools. My original intent, although I could do it with my eyes closed, wasn't just to play D1 football as a long-snapper. Ideally, I wanted to start on the offensive line (specifically an "offensive tackle" position) but I *was certain* my long-snapping abilities could get me onto a squad at the very least.

Well, regardless if you ever engaged in an athletics recruiting process or not, let me tell you how many collegiate programs and coaching staffs do it: they make you feel *wanted*. But the really best teams don't just make you *feel* wanted—they convey how much they *need* you and your skill set, and map out a plan for how you can help them succeed.

Were there elements of this strategy from the aforementioned schools, such as Minnesota and Michigan? Sure. But none of them made the kind of effort as a school that hit way closer to home: Northwestern University located just outside of Chicago.

It was around my junior season that I began serious talks with their coaching staff about attending Northwestern after graduating from Mount Carmel. The one thing I knew *before* talking with coaches and players was that they didn't have the most successful or well-known football program in the country. Nothing wrong with that! Northwestern *is* known for solid academics and for preparing students for a solid career and life after school—more than enough to make up for a lackluster football program.

But what I learned *after* talking to coaches and players was that the program wasn't lackluster at all. In fact, it was the total opposite of lackluster—even if the win/loss column didn't always reflect it.

Throughout my junior year in high school, I learned more about the program, yes, but also saw enough promise for their team in terms of what they were building. In other words, going to one of the big-name powerhouse schools like Michigan might've made sense to most. It would have been the next best step—like seeing an easy move in a game of checkers. But I am someone who has always been more inclined to play chess, so I looked for a program that exhibited strategy for three to five moves ahead at a time.

That line of thinking led me to Northwestern. I saw how I could not only fit in as a freshman but how I could grow *with them* in the years ahead, as the coaching staff truly cast a vision for the future of football at the university.

During my junior year, I made a soft commitment to attend Northwestern and play for head coach Gary Barnett. It was kind of a funny thing because they had just finished up the year with a 3-7 record. That's just three wins amid seven losses . . . but again, I knew what they were building internally, and I wanted to be a part of it. And Gary Barnett was at the helm. He had ALL his players, his recruits, and the recruit's families bought in to "Expect Victory" and that he would take the Wildcats to Pasadena to play in the Rose Bowl. He set a vision, sold that vision to everybody that would listen, and told people about it until they truly believed. Gary Barnett was a master at building a vision from afar, and knowing what it would take to get there and I was hooked! I only told the people closest to me: my family, the coaching staff at Mount Carmel, and one of my closest friends: Kevin Dowling.

Yep, Kevin was one of the only ones who knew about my decision to attend Northwestern for the longest time. It's cool knowing that, up until his death, he kept that secret of mine until he passed away, which says one more thing about Kevin and his loyalty. When I *did* commit during the fall of our senior year, I had just attended a Northwestern vs. Wisconsin football game. The final score was 35-0 . . . Northwestern. The tide was turning, and I was ready to dive in. I verbally committed to the school after that game, making that secret more public.

And when I told others of my decision to attend an up-and-coming Division 1 football program, I made sure they knew I wouldn't just be playing for myself. I'd be playing for two. In other words, if he couldn't be there with me in a *physical* sense, I knew Kevin would be joining me at Northwestern in a spiritual and emotional sense. I couldn't wait for both of us to travel downtown together to Northwestern's campus. We'd be trading in super burritos for a shot at playing football at the highest collegiate level.

Everyone else in and around Mount Carmel was thrilled about my decision to play at Northwestern. Obviously, it was close enough to where they could attend most of the games. But they also understood the vision for the program well into the future and were excited to buy all the Northwestern gear and cheer me on from the proverbial sidelines.

After I verbally committed, and after Northwestern pummeled Wisconsin, they went to the Rose Bowl at the end of the football season. It was a tell-tale sign they were improving as a program, and I couldn't wait to join. Some people around Mount Carmel joked with me, saying I only wanted to play at Northwestern because they made it to the Rose Bowl that year. But I knew, just like Kevin knew my junior year, that I committed *far prior* to the Rose Bowl because I saw something special brewing that I wanted to be a part of.

Northwestern's campus was about an hour away from my family's home in Oak Lawn (including typical Chicago traffic). Although I'd be "leaving the nest" as an 18-year-old kid, I did like knowing my family would be just down the road if I ever needed anything major. But they were so great about giving me space to flourish on my own as a freshman. To this day, I am forever grateful for all the sacrifices my parents, Jack and Karen, and my sweet sister, Carrie, made all those years coming to my football games and traveling with me to college camps, etc. In the end, I received a full scholarship to play football at Northwestern. So many people hear about "full-ride" scholarships and think it's pretty cool that the student doesn't have to pay for school, which is true. But you know who else that full ride is a blessing to? The family who sacrificed many years to help their loved one get to that place. I'll always be thankful to mine.

Now, when I say "flourish on my own as a freshman" I really just mean the time and space it took for me to figure out life as a student-athlete. I don't know if there was much flourishing until my sophomore year or so, as freshman year is such a learning curve for anyone—*especially* the student-athlete juggling sports and academics.

A quality education from Mount Carmel prepared me for most of my college education, but Northwestern isn't exactly a cakewalk. Unlike some bigger state schools, the staff and faculty at Northwestern don't so highly prioritize sports in addition to their expectations for you in the classroom. Therefore, everyone is held to the same standards in the classroom—whether an athlete or not. Looking back now, I'm so grateful that was the case, even though it was a pretty difficult reality to wade through shortly after arriving on campus.

It was class and studying all morning (until about 2 p.m.) and then practicing and watching films all afternoon until dinner time, then going to study hall until 10 pm (then going back to the dorm to study more).

Wash, rinse, and repeat for pretty much the entire duration of my freshman year at Northwestern.

Were those first few months as a freshman, in the fall of 1996, a bit of a roller coaster? Out of my comfort zone? Stretching me in ways I hadn't experienced before? "Yes" to all the above. But for the first time in my life, it was where I started taking *ownership* of my life, schedule, dreams, and aspirations. In other words, that freshman year is where my "Snap & Go" mentality sprouted out of the ground, even if the seeds had been planted years prior by individuals such as my parents, Grandma Betty, and Kevin in high school.

My whole family came to those first football games that fall, and it was such a blast to maintain the Chicago connection. Even more fun was just living just north of downtown in one of the best cities in the world.

Is Chicago perfect? Of course not. No place is. But if you take *modern-day* Chicago into account, you might simply think of a dense, over-popularized city with a violence problem. I really hope you don't see Chicago as just that, even though violence *is* a problem in this big city. No, that aspect is just a part of the whole. When you think of images or videos you see of Chicago, you might think about a bunch of homes that are close together—specifically on the south side of Chicago, I know those kinds of homes and communities well. The truth is that living in close proximity to one another can be as life-giving as much as it can present the opportunity to hurt others.

Whether you live in Chicago, another big city, or a small rural town in the Midwest . . . I hope you always find ways to lean toward the "life-giving" side of building and maintaining a high-quality culture and community.

One of the ways I was exposed to giving back to the community during my freshman year at Northwestern was when our head coach, Gary Barnett, encouraged us to get involved with a local nonprofit organization to serve on a regular basis. It may have seemed like *one more thing* to tack onto our crazy student-athlete plates, but man am I glad he encouraged us to do so.

For me, it was the *Boys & Girls Club of Chicago*, and the times I'd spend with those sweet kids made all the hardship of my day-to-day schedule fade into the distance. Those moments helped me realize the influence I could have on a new generation of kids in Chicago. Even if it wasn't *hundreds* of kids I'd spend time with, just giving a few of them my time and attention was enough to brighten their day and give them hope and encouragement for the weeks and months ahead.

So if you want to talk about planting seeds, I think *that* is how it's done. It's a slow process, but the impact is long-lasting. There's no "quick fix" to any of Chicago's problems or any other city's problems in America, but patience and persistence *are* a part of the solution.

Individuals like Coach Barnett instilled that idea and principle into my mind as a freshman, and it's how I knew I wanted to impact the city for good for as long as I was living there. The roots of those experiences to serve, in honesty, partly led to me writing this book. I *know* that I am still in a leadership position, and I *know* that others are looking up to me whether I realize it or not.

It's just one more example that Kevin taught me before he left: that others *are* watching, so live your life accordingly.

Walking onto campus that freshman year at Northwestern, I knew for a fact I'd be watched playing the game I love. Watched by coaches. Watched by players. And watched by the faithful Wildcat fans in the stands. But it's funny how the kids, through a program like Boys & Girls Club of Chicago, became my most important audience. Why? Because they're the ones who one day might, in the words of the musical *Hamilton*, "Blow us all away."

Future generations are the ones that have *many more* snaps to go than us, so how are we setting them up accordingly? It's the kind of question I would end up revisiting in the years to come, especially with my own two kiddos, but first . . . my time at Northwestern wasn't quite through. In fact, it was just beginning!

That 6'7" football player had surpassed 300 lbs and had the whole rest of his playing career ahead of him. A full-ride scholarship. A quality education. And a loving family just down the road. Yes, once I got squared away on the football team and settled into my local Chicago community, I felt excited about the next few years.

But if you know anything about the game of football, it's when you become complacent that you're susceptible to a hit from the blind side. And even though that "blindside hit" *would* come, all I was worried about was my current job to do. And I was more determined in my life than ever for one thing: perfection at my craft.

6

I f you've never met someone who grew up in Chicago in the late '80s or early '90s, allow me to be the first—it'd be an honor! Yet if you *do* know someone who grew up in Chicago around that time frame, you can reach out and fact-check what I'm about to say:

Eighty-seven percent of boys growing up in Chicago had a poster of Michael Jordan hanging up in their room.

Alright . . . is there any scientific research behind that statistic? No. In fact, I just made that number up. (Like a decent amount of statistics). But I said it *as* fact to make a greater point: Michael Jordan was the apple of every Chicago kid's eye in the late '80s and early '90s— it really didn't matter if you were a boy or girl because everyone in Chicago land was utterly infatuated with the guy. And for good reason!

I only included 87% of *boys* because I was one, and if you *do* fact-check with one of your friends who grew up in Chicago around that time, they very well might fall in that 13% that didn't follow the Chicago Bulls or their epic NBA Championship runs year after year. Regardless, Michael Jordan is one of the most famous individuals not just in sports, but in the world. And it's because he's known for way more than just winning championships. In Chapter 1 of this book, I made mention of MJ's *mentality* when on the court.

Michael would take every circumstance surrounding a game—in and outside of the arena—and use those circumstances to fuel his game and competitiveness. It's that kind of mentality that was on display for us Chicago kids night after night and was inevitably on display for the world to see when the Bulls reached a championship stage every year.

And in 2020, while most of the world was in lockdown mode—inside their homes due to a global pandemic—one of the most popular ESPN documentaries to ever air on TV was streamed into millions of homes. *The Last Dance* followed Michael's rise from a humble high school player in North Carolina to a cut-throat NBA MVP that absolutely demolished the competition—night after night, year after year.

Therefore, the world now has a little better idea of what MJ and those Bulls teams meant to our city. And although our family didn't have season tickets to Bulls games, you better believe we had the Bulls on TV a good amount of the time. For a family that spent a lot of time around the football field, we still loved watching those Bulls teams compete for year-in and year out.

But there was one year when the TV wasn't enough. When I had an opportunity to see Michael in the flesh, I took it. Yet it wasn't at Chicago Stadium (aka Madhouse on Madison), it was actually in the streets of

Chicago—after the Bulls had just won their first of what would become *six* NBA titles throughout the '90s. It was 1991, and I was in the eighth grade.

The city of Chicago, in welcoming the Bulls and their championship trophy, had basically shut down the city for a parade that was centered around Grant Park—right in the heart of downtown Chicago. It was evident that thousands of people would line the streets to go see the parade, and downtown would be, similar to the Bulls arena, a true madhouse.

As for my friends and me? Days before the Bulls won the championship and scheduled their parade, we decided to go fishing at a nearby pond—a place we frequented often. Our parents knew whenever we'd go fishing, that's where they could find us.

And to this day . . . it's a small regret of mine that we followed through with that plan.

We *did* go fishing that day. And we *did* watch the Bulls parade—it was just on my friend's little living room TV. It's something we laugh about to this day because my parents are *convinced* we went full Ferris Bueller and bolted downtown to watch the celebration. (I promise we didn't, Mom!)

But the fact of the matter is that every Chicago citizen wanted to be downtown that day. There was a buzz and an energy that started a fire in Chicago sports fans everywhere for close to a decade. It's wild to think about, as I'm hard-pressed to think anybody like Michael will ever come along again in *any* sport and have the kind of impact he did on a game . . . let alone a city.

So fast-forward to me from 1991 to 1996. Another athlete was about to make his presence known in downtown Chicago. And where Michael Jordan stood at a towering 6'6", this *new* player stood at 6'7"—so you could say he was kind of a bigger deal than Michael.

I'll stop there. Yes, I'm the *other* athlete in downtown Chicago circa 1996. And no, I was *not* a bigger deal than Michael. Far from it. It's funny to think about—kids all across the city (and country by that point) had giant posters in their rooms of Michael's famous "Air Jordan" dunk from the free throw line. I'm not sure they would have gotten as excited about a Jack Harnedy poster from Northwestern University—in a goofy three-point stance sticking his rear end in the air. But that's the position I found myself in for about four glorious years in downtown Chicago, and I'm grateful for every one of them.

By 1996, the Bulls were working on their *fourth* championship (which they'd go on to win) and were establishing their dominance. Northwestern football? Not so much. But there *was* progress.

All of those conversations alongside coaches at Northwestern—where they'd cast a vision for the future of their program—would slowly come to fruition, and I was just thrilled to be a part of it. It was my first time living on my own, and even though it was a mere hour away from my home in Oak Lawn, it felt like a world away. A beautiful world. And a world that would set the stage for the rest of my life.

During that fall of 1996, I arrived on campus and knew it was where I was meant to be almost immediately. I say "almost" because college is a learning experience for any teenage kid. Northwestern's campus is just north of downtown in the suburb of Evanston, and it is *gorgeous*. The grounds crew does an amazing job every year of maintaining and keeping a beautiful outward façade with its greenery and cleanliness. But Northwestern is obviously more than a façade. Inside those buildings are some of the brightest students in America, and it was humbling to rub shoulders with many of those individuals in my first few weeks in class. However, as a freshman football player on a full-ride scholarship, there were different shoulders. I was really ready to work alongside—my teammates. And when it wasn't the guy next to me, it was doing everything in my power to prepare for the opportunity . . . the opportunity to knock the guy in front of me to the ground, and do it with the same intensity that Michael Jordan did just down the road.

OK, so the basketball-to-football analogy doesn't really translate. Michael wasn't tasked with shoving guys to the ground as much as he was getting to the basket. But again, many of us channeled a "Michael

Mentality" on the field, and who knows—maybe it's a small reason why our Northwestern program finally started to experience success in the '90s after a few decades of Big 10 mediocrity.

I'll never forget the first time I walked out onto the grass at Dyche Stadium as a *player*. Dyche Stadium had astroturf that was as soft as concrete and if you fell down, it was as if a million razorblades sliced you all at once. If I'm honest, I'm still trying to heal my turf burn from early in my Northwestern career. Thankfully, the stadium transitioned to Ryan Field (with soft long grass) during my second year at Northwestern. I had sat in the stands of that place for a few games before, mostly when I was being recruited by Northwestern. But when I got to campus as a student and entered the locker room as an athlete, I knew it was about to be me and my teammates stepping onto the field on Saturdays.

All I'd have to do is something I'd been doing for about a decade: utilizing my God-given talent, putting forth my best effort, and leaving it all out on the field.

I say "about a decade" because I actually didn't start playing football until the sixth grade. Until then, it was a lot of soccer and baseball, and I'm grateful for that fact because my dad *definitely* could have gotten me started in football earlier—yet he knew how physical the game is (as society is becoming more aware of football-induced head trauma) in addition to the mental toll. I'm thankful because I never got burned out on the game, and I know it's because I was able to play multiple sports, start football a little later in childhood, and ultimately put more emphasis on academics among other activities. (Like hitting up Burrito Station with my friends).

But once I *did* start playing football, I was hooked. And I know that my dad was pretty pumped to get me out on the gridiron as well. As an assistant coach of Mount Carmel at the time, my dad had all the knowledge of the game I could've asked for as a kid. Maybe, more importantly, he had the connections to help me become a prominent high school player, and one of those connections changed the course of my playing career.

In sixth grade, my father introduced me to a man who had been a Division 1 long-snapper and was now a coach at a local elementary school. My father knew, if I was to have any future in football (whether after high school or beyond) that this *one skill* could get me there. My dad talked to me about the uniqueness of long-snapping, and how difficult the skill is to perfect. But this coach that he got me connected with walked me through the mechanics of snapping a football between my legs with speed and accuracy, and I was enthralled.

It was an action I could practice in my spare time at home (flinging the ball at a wall 45 feet behind me) or on the sidelines with a friend at practice. *Repetition* is what got me to the point of proficiency in middle school, but *discipline* was the core of what led to my long-snapping prowess in high school.

However, where this one skill would inevitably set me apart from other high school recruits in the Chicago area, it was simply a position on the offensive line that I loved playing.

Again, this goes back to the role of "in the trenches" alongside your brothers in battle. The kind of grind you only fully understand if you've ever gotten in a three-point stance and heard the quarterback hike the ball before exploding into the man in front of you —a few hundred pounds of football equipment, flesh, sweat, and terrible-smelling practice jerseys clashing against each other at full force. And yes . . . a few of those pounds attributed to Burrito Station down the road.

Something about that offensive line unit is what I loved being a part of. Don't get me wrong—long-snapping was *fun* because I got to touch the ball for a few plays every game, which is not something every offensive lineman gets to do. But helping lay a foundation for our team's success is what I really loved, and that foundation starts on the offensive line.

Walking on the field at Dyche Stadium as a freshman at Northwestern, I knew I was a part of a program that was in the process of rebuilding its foundation, and it meant success for years to come.

And guess what—playing on the offensive line *and* long-snapping . . . I'd get to do both! It was part of my recruiting process, as the coaches knew my size, strength, knowledge of the game, and *desire* to do both was there. They assured me I would have an opportunity, through practice and a little brotherly competition, to earn a spot playing on the offensive line in addition to long-snapping for the team.

And for my first couple of years at Northwestern, that was my reality! I got a good amount of in-game playing time after my true freshman year as a redshirt. But there was one position that was solely *mine* . . .

It was all thanks to some wisdom and foresight on my dad's behalf, and the guidance of a friend, mentor, and coach to help get me there. By 1996, I could long snap a ball between my legs with the same accuracy and precision that MJ could pass a basketball behind his back. It helped me lock down the long-snapping role as a freshman, and it felt amazing to be able to contribute to Northwestern's new foundation right away.

Snap, block, and cause some chaos. That little formula is simplifying it just a *little*, but it is the job of a long-snapper, in short.

Snapping I had down. I simply had to walk out onto a field, stand over that prolate spheroid shape of brown leather, and rifle it back to the punter in less than a second's time so that he could punt the ball downfield to the opposing returner. Yep, snapping came as naturally to me as eating cereal with a spoon, but there was a *different* kind of learning curve during game days at Ryan Field.

The University of Michigan, the University of Wisconsin, and The Ohio State University . . . other Big 10 schools in our conference, many of whom had recruited me while at Mount Carmel, were standing on the other side of that snap. And trust me . . . these weren't the same kind of kids I was up against while at Mount Carmel.

During that first year, I learned from the absolute best in the business: Defensive Player of the Year, Linebacker Pat Fitzgerald.

As a redshirt, your sole job is to prepare the first string for the upcoming game on Saturday. As a scout team player, you took on the identity of the opponent. Fitz taught me, from day one, that there was NO slacking while on the field. He went all out, all the time . . . and he expected it from every teammate. He never took a play off, preparing and working harder than anybody I had ever seen. He taught me firsthand that you play like you practice, which is a lesson I would take with me for years to come.

Although I towered over kids in high school from a height and weight standpoint, Division 1 college football pretty much consists of 6'5"+ young men across the board. I was no longer the exception, but the rule. Thus, "blocking" these guys took a little more preparation and intensity than before, and the result truly *was* some chaos on whatever Big 10 field we happened to be playing on any given Saturday.

There weren't enough super burritos that could have prepared me for that task—just focus in the weight room, preparation in the film room, and a coaching staff that trusted me to do my job week-in and week-out. *That* was my formula for success at Northwestern. And even though *I* experienced a decent amount of success on the offensive line and as a long-snapper, our team wasn't experiencing the same kind of *consistent* success that we all expected out of ourselves.

9-3 (my redshirt year). 5-7. 3-9. 8-4.

We weren't exactly the Chicago Bulls, but in my first year at Northwestern, we finished as Big Ten Champions at 9-3. We had a slight setback in year two with a 5-7 record. Successful enough for a D1 school to compete in a tough conference? Absolutely. Enough success to meet our high standard of competing for a national championship? Not quite. So you can imagine our team's collective response that third year when *3-9* was our season's outcome. Ouch!

Talk about a mental and emotional setback. The year we went 3-9, it was like the foundation we had worked hard to build was showing some serious cracks. To fix those cracks that started to reveal themselves, the program moved in a different direction and hired a new head coach.

Throughout my recruiting process, all I had known was Coach Gary Barnett at the helm. I was sad to see him go, especially because I was entering the back half of my playing career and didn't know what the future would hold for me and our team. I loved the energy, passion, charisma, and everything else Coach Barnett brought to our team, and brought out in me, and I hated to see that go.

Well, turns out that the future contained a man by the name of Randy Walker. He was joining us from his time at a smaller school a couple of states over at the University of Miami (Ohio).

Upon his arrival, we all met Coach Walker he was a great guy right off the bat, but he was going to bring a different mentality to our team. As sad as it was to see Coach Barnett leave, we knew a change might be for the better, and maybe this promising young coach would be the one to help us fix those cracks in the foundation, and continue building the basis for a successful future. The transition was tough for many, but if you embraced Coach Walker's hard-nosed, hard work, gritty attitude, you would be accepted by him and his staff.

We got along well. And he appreciated my leadership from an upper-classmen standpoint. He let me know my presence was needed amid the coaching transition, and that I'd be a big part of our success during that first 1999 season of his.

There was only one problem . . . Coach Walker didn't like that, in addition to my normal long-snapping duties, I also played on the offensive line.

7

The Big House. The Horseshoe. Happy Valley. If you are at all familiar with college football, you know each of these names is associated with big-time college football stadiums. The Big House is where the University of Michigan plays. The Horseshoe belongs to their rival, Ohio State. And Happy Valley is home to the Penn State Nittany Lions. You also might notice something about these schools . . . they're all in the same conference.

Now, it goes without saying that Ryan Field in the heart of Chicago doesn't solicit the same kind of 100,000-ticket crowds that those schools might have in attendance at a game. (A big reason for those giant stadiums built in the mid-20th century, was that they wanted to give as many people who didn't have TVs an opportunity to come to watch a game). But don't count our school out—there is as much spirit in the Northwestern fanbase as anywhere else, but our program just doesn't have as much success as those other schools have had . . . so kudos to them for creating an awesome culture throughout the decades.

Side: As of this writing, Northwestern has plans for an incredible new football facility. If you find yourself with a ticket to a game there someday, let me know! I'd love to come to say hey and maybe even sign this book :)

But again, although I had a chance to join multiple other schools—from Oklahoma to Nebraska, Wisconsin to Michigan, Ohio State, and Minnesota among others. But I loved what Northwestern was building—even to this day! The blend of athletic prowess and academic success is ultimately what I was looking for, and I wouldn't trade my decision for anything.

In addition, a huge plus of playing at Northwestern was knowing I'd get to travel *to* those giant stadiums across the country — experiences that I'll hold onto for a lifetime.

It's the craziest thing running out of those tunnels to hear 80,000-100,000 people cheering at some of those Division I stadiums. The noise is deafening—a blend of screaming fans and collegiate bands playing school fight songs. The "Imperial March" from *Star Wars* is one that sticks out—a favorite of bands to play when the opposing team steps onto the field. But everything that happens before the game isn't as crazy as the pandemonium *within* the game. I had the joy of playing on the offensive line for Northwestern, where we heard those crowds reach insane decibel levels, making it hard to hear your own thoughts. However, I obviously had the honor of long-snapping in those same environments . . . where the weirdest thing would happen.

Happy Valley specifically comes to mind for some reason. Again, the home of Penn State boasts one of the most intimidating environments to play a football game in. And

I'll never forget my time playing on that field. As a long-snapper, I'd fling the ball between my legs like I had done thousands of times before. When I'd look up and release downfield to go cause some chaos, it's like silence would come over the crowd. Again, this would happen regardless of most stadiums, but there's something about that specific environment—when "Happy Valley" goes silent while the punter's kick goes nearly 90 feet in the air.

It was one of the joys of playing that position, and I look back fondly on those moments . . . when it was just me running down a field at full speed, with not a care in the world but pursuing a punt returner with full force. Another joy is looking back on those players I got to go up against. A few come to mind—two of them were some of the fastest returners that I remember watching step onto a football field.

The first was a player from the University of Nebraska named Bobby Newcombe. You can look up "Bobby Newcombe Punt Return" on YouTube to get a glimpse of how dangerous that guy was with a football in his hands. The odds of my 6'7," 300lb frame running that guy down were slim-to-none, but I'd be darned if I didn't try. The second player I vividly remember pursuing was someone a bit more well-known than Bobby, but just as fast and athletic. The reason Charles Woodson comes to my mind is that, well, he won the Heisman Trophy in 1997 and went on to have an incredible NFL career. He was just a freak on the football field, and we all spent as much time chasing him down as we did marveling at his athletic ability. The third player that comes to mind, for me, in my career doubles as one of my most vivid memories in college.

It happened against the University of Tennessee in the Citrus Bowl in 1997. Tennessee has a wonderful fan base, and as Tennessee's team enters the stadium, their band plays "Rocky Top" and everything about the scene screams college football. But the real reason I remember that game so vividly is because of their quarterback at the time . . . you might have heard of him: Peyton Manning.

There was just something about watching Peyton come out of the tunnel, hearing the crowd go wild, but examining how he carried himself in the aftermath—both before, during, and after the game was over. Now, if you know anything about college or pro football and its history, you know the last name "Manning" carries some weight. Peyton was more or less born-and-bred to compete at the highest level of football, and his demeanor showed it. I'm sure I'm not the only one who was affected by his style on the field. You couldn't help but respect and admire him then, and he's kept up a cool persona for himself to this day. A true class act who has had an awesome impact on the game of football.

Guys like Woodson and Manning made headlines in the mid-to-late '90s, but guys like me were just trying to soak up each minute of our playing careers, and maybe get a crack at the next level. While those guys were busy slicing through opposing defenses and offenses, I was just focused on the job I had come to do at Northwestern.

With any position in football, there is little room for error. Quarterbacks throw incomplete passes and interceptions. Wide receivers drop balls thrown to them. And linebackers miss tackles and assignments from time to time. It's all just how the game goes. But there is one position in football where there is *very little* room for error: the long-snapping position.

And when a long-snapper does commit an error, you will notice it as a spectator. Errors from a long-snapper might look a little like this:

- Punter has to shuffle to his right or left to receive the snap.

- The ball/snap goes OVER the punter's head, and the chaos begins behind the line of scrimmage.

- Ball is wobbly on the way to the punter.

- Ball doesn't get to the punter fast enough — increasing the chances of a blocked punt.

Just a few of the ways a long-snapper might "fail" at his job—again, there really is little room for error. When do you know a long-snapper is doing his job? That's the flip side of the position itself . . . when a long-snapper is doing his job, you won't think twice about it. In other words, it's kind of a "no news is good news" situation on any given sideline.

With all of that being said, it's pretty important for a long-snapper to eat, drink, and breathe long-snapping throughout the season. For a long snapper to divert his attention elsewhere? Well, that might only distract him from performing that one task with excellence. And, heaven forbid, an offensive lineman (who doubles as the team's long-snapper) breaks a finger and can no longer perform his long-snapping duties.

The latter is where Coach Randy Walker was coming from when he voiced that I make an important decision.

"Jack, you're going to have to make a choice. You can stick with the offensive line, but I can't guarantee you much playing time there. Or you can focus solely on long-snapping."

I wish I could say it was a more difficult decision for me, as I really did love playing on the offensive line. However, I understood where he was coming from. There were younger offensive linemen he wanted to get in the mix, and I just wasn't going to be a part of his renewed vision for the team three to four years out. And so I turned my attention to not just long-snapping, but the other position I held dear to my heart: short-snapping.

Now, throughout this book I have made little mention of short-snapping—partly because this role has been implied, but partly because long-snapping is a little more difficult. However, both are incredibly important in the context of football and special teams.

Short-snapping is the "field goal" version of a punt. Short-snappers need to deliver the ball quickly and accurately to the holder's hands before they place the football on the ground for a kicker to attempt a field goal. So when I say punting is a little more difficult, I just mean that the distance between the snapper and punter is farther, yet you still need to deliver the ball right at his belly button. But with short-snapping, you are the first of three performed actions that need to go perfectly: the snap, the hold, and the kick. If the first of those actions is off, the last two actions will likely go poorly.

Both actions are difficult. Both actions I excelled in. And if the rest of my career at Northwestern would be marked by my success in those areas, then I vowed to do everything in my power to excel as a long-snapper and short-snapper.

It was my attempt to make the best of that last year or so at Northwestern, but what I didn't know is how much it would set me up for success later in life. (More on that later).

As my senior year approached, I poured everything into the game and my responsibilities as the long-snapper and short-snapper for Northwestern. We had a new head coach Randy Walker and I knew he was leaning on older guys like myself for leadership roles on the team. While playing Division I football, you quickly realize that 90% of the game actually occurs *off* the field, and the other 10% of success occurs on the field. If you take care of business with the 90% beforehand, the other 10% is just execution. That 10%, for me, was doing what I did best: snapping a football between my legs, blocking out the chaos, and focusing on the person in front of me.

As for the 90% before any given game, I was focused on helping my teammates become better in the process. Many of them looked up to me as a leader, so I did my best to help them prepare for games in the weeks leading up to Saturday. We watched films together, studied defenses together, and put in effort in the weight room together. The result was strong team unity, and we felt really good heading into Coach Walker's second season as our head coach.

As a team, we were rolling on all cylinders, and I had fully settled into my role as a snapper—although I didn't have another on-field role, I knew I had a lot to offer the team off the field as well.

Therefore, you can imagine my disappointment when my on-field role was not just threatened, but in actual jeopardy.

I'll never forget the day at practice when my playing career changed for good. In fact, you might say it was "the beginning of the end" of my football career, and it came as just as much of a shock to me as it did to others on the team.

For three years straight, I had a firm grip on the short-snapping role at Northwestern. But heading into my final season, I knew there was a teammate a couple of years younger than me who was the next man up if something happened to me like a freak injury. Well, what happened on a summer day during practice seemed as much of an accident as an injury would have at that time. It was like one day I was doing what I had been doing for years —snap, hold, kick —and the next day something just felt off.

Not many people in the country were better at me than snapping that piece of leather, but in terms of short-snapping . . . All of a sudden, I got in my head. It happened once, and I thought, "That was weird," but when it happened two more times, and then five . . . a few coaches took notice.

"What's going on, Harnedy?"

I had no idea. I tried to snap the ball at a longer distance, as if to a punter through my long-snapping duties and had no problem there. But with *short-snapping,* it's like the shorter distance actually hindered me even more.

The coaches looked on curiously as I tried to nail down the snap to the holder, and I felt their eyes bearing down on me. Off to the sideline, I noticed the kid who was a couple of years behind me. Even though I knew he wasn't better than me at short-snapping, I knew he'd more than jump at a chance to take over the position.

That's when Coach Walker gave him a chance—a little window of an opportunity to show he could do something that I all-of-a-sudden could not do.

Some people call this phenomenon "the yips" because it's a seemingly small thing that affects the mind and body, and it's the only real explanation I have for whatever happened that day. It was a combination of me not performing the simple (but very important!) task, and another, younger athlete seizing his opportunity.

And he *did* seize the opportunity. And it *did* happen that fast—one summer day at practice led to me losing my short-snapping role at Northwestern University.

I was embarrassed and a bit shaken up. Even thinking about it today takes me to a tough place, as it's a huge moment in my life where not just my position but my *identity* was put in question. Until Coach Walker came to town, I was an offensive lineman, short *and* long-snapper, and overall decent collegiate football player. Within a matter of months, my role was reduced to mere long-snapper. And that's when I had to make a decision. Would I let that one role define me, or would I persevere through adversity and undertake the *other* role I was being asked of: a senior leader for the rest of my teammates?

The decision I made that summer was to own the coach's decision to go with the other short snapper and assume my two new roles as leader and long-snapper. Before I go any further, please know I don't have animosity for Coach Walker or any other coach in choosing another player to take on short-snapping duties. I believe it was a bit of a pride thing, and definitely an identity issue — one that was tough at the moment, but I'm glad I went through it because it taught me a lot about facing adversity in the workplace (which is what Division I athletics feels like) and boy am I glad I had that opportunity!

Because it *was* an opportunity to learn and grow. In the aftermath of that decision, I pursued the rest of my senior year with intentionality and focused on those two roles —leader and long-snapper—because our team and coaching staff was counting on me to do so. Besides, if I took the long-snapping role as seriously as possible, I might catch serious attention from the NFL and have a shot at playing at the next level.

But even if I didn't play in the NFL, my time at Northwestern would be marked by a guy who gave his all to a program that was growing and had a bright future ahead. After all, that's why I came to Northwestern in the first place, and it's part of the reason I chose to honor those who helped me get there.

Everyone from my parents to my sister, to Grandma Betty, to Kevin Dowling, and the whole Mount Carmel community. They knew I was more than just Jack Harnedy, the long *or* short-snapper.

They saw me as a leader, and so I would round out my time at Northwestern as just that. Little did I know it would catapult me into a future filled with similar opportunities —opportunities that didn't look exactly like I thought they would, but opportunities that would make me the man I am today.

8

Preparing for an NFL career is a wild thing, because it starts *years* prior to draft day or getting signed by an NFL team —it often starts in high school or even middle school.

Because the NFL contains such a small percentage of football players in America, there is just a different kind of talent you need to stick out. And if you ask anyone who has ever played with an NFL-type talent, they'll tell you that the signs were there around middle or high school.

It's a combination of size, athleticism, talent, and knowledge of the game. If you have a blend of all four characteristics, you have a much better chance than someone with just three of those tools to play at the highest possible level. In high school, I felt pretty confident in regard to all four characteristics, but college is where the NFL talent is separated from the rest. And if there was one phrase that made all the difference, I would say "hard work" separates those who build on the four characteristics, and those who let them remain stagnant.

During my time at Northwestern, I knew if I could increase my size (in the weight room), athleticism (in practice), talent (in-game performance), and knowledge (in the film room), I would put myself in a position to impress NFL scouts and begin my professional football career.

It was part of the thing that kept me motivated during my final season at Northwestern—especially when I lost my short-snapping role, I decided to set my sights on contributing as a captain on the team and preparing myself for the next level.

The NFL tryouts came and went. I had great discussions with some scouts, and even an agent to help me in the process. I was doing all the right things and everything I could to position myself for the moment my name might get called to an NFL roster . . . and then came the unfortunate feedback that altered my NFL dream.

In so many words, I had representatives from a team or two affirm my athleticism, talent, and knowledge of the game—three of the four characteristics needed to play in the NFL. But that fourth one? In their eyes, I took size a bit too far. My 6'7" height hadn't changed in years, but I was told that a 300-pound-plus long snapper in the NFL wasn't ideal. In their eyes, I would need to get down between 225-250 pounds if I wanted a shot at the pros. For a kid who had given the game so much until that point, and had taken a beating on a week-to-week basis for so many years, I knew this next phase was just not in the cards.

A tough pill to swallow? Absolutely. A few too many super burritos in high school? Perhaps. But I wouldn't trade ANY of those burritos and memories shared with Kevin and my high school buddies for the world.

Now, of course, my circumstances were about way more than super burritos. My playing weight was largely the result of playing offensive line during my first few years at Northwestern, and 300 lbs for a Division I offensive lineman was more of the rule, not the exception. So when my offensive lineman weight made an impact on my prospects of playing long-snapper in the NFL, I understood where those scouts and teams were coming from.

But for me, in that season of life, I was able to take a step back, evaluate my career prospects, and decide that football wasn't it —the new plan was to fully utilize my college education and get a job upon graduation.

And if you think this is where my story turns from exciting NFL prospects to a boring 9-5 job, please think again.

In fact, this is actually a turning point in this book where I highlight a true "launch point" in my life, and shift into a phase of my life and story that I believe is directly applicable to your own life and work journey.

It's not lost on me that many readers of this book, yourself included, won't be able to relate to the life and times of a Division I college long-snapper. But the reason I went into such detail about my past is so that I could hopefully encourage you in the present, and set you up for future success.

The "Snap & Go" mindset I began this book with is what carried me through college, yes, but it's also what set me up for a successful path *following* my time playing football. It's the kind of mindset that I think can help anyone — no matter what industry or area of expertise you might occupy.

Whether you're in high school, a recent college graduate, a young professional, a tenured businessman or woman, or leading a team of any kind . . . this is the point in the book where I ask you to stand over your own prolate spheroid shape of leather, trust in your God-given ability, and step into the good work you were born to do. Because the thing I would find very quickly after my time with the Northwestern football team is this: *what* we're doing each day in this life doesn't matter nearly as much as *how* we do it.

It's what my parents taught me years ago—in a humble home on the south side of Chicago.

It's what my grandmother, Betty Harnedy, exemplified each day of her career alongside so many.

It's what my best friend, Kevin Dowling, taught me and so many others about playing until the final whistle.

And it's what my coaching staff and teammates displayed, in the trenches each week, while playing collegiate football at Northwestern University.

If my first 22 years on this earth were spent as a sponge soaking up all the great wisdom and lessons learned from those around me, I felt like my time post-grad was a time to wring out what I had learned to those around me. The only question was what I'd do and where I'd do it. But again, no matter the answer to those questions, I knew one thing wasn't in question . . . *how* I'd attack each day. It was kind of a promise I made to myself in that season of life, and I hope you can do the same after putting down this book.

After donning the Northwestern black and purple for the final time, and turning my tassel to accept a Master's Degree in Integrated Marketing Communications, there were friends and family members that were curious about what I'd do next. For a while, their guess was as good as mine. But in time, I got connected to an individual who told me about an opportunity with a company that wasn't even on my radar upon graduation. The opportunity sounded, to me, similar to when I committed to Northwestern in the first place—not the most glamorous option but one with a growing company that had a great vision for where it was heading.

The company was Rubbermaid—a manufacturer and distributor of many products you have used before, even if you didn't realize or think about it. From trash cans to storage bins, to food containers . . . they are leaders in their industry, and from my college graduate point of view, they came out of nowhere.

I received an email from a representative at Rubbermaid, and he told me how a few members of their team had followed the Northwestern football team and my career. That was obviously a shock, but it was cool that someone in a professional setting noticed all the hard work I was putting into my role year after year.

This individual told me about a new program they were starting at Rubbermaid called the "Phoenix Program" that would position young professionals for a long-term career in the area of consumer packaged goods (CPG). Of course, that term was pretty foreign to me at the time, but once he described the nature of their business, I was intrigued. At the time, the other opportunity I was considering was with an advertising agency in New York. It would have been a higher-paying role than the Rubbermaid gig, and most of my friends in college *were* pursuing such roles with bigger-name companies.

It was reminiscent of a decision I had had to make before: go play in front of a hundred thousand screaming fans, where there was decorated history and athletic prestige, or to a smaller program with a good culture and growing program?

Well, choosing the latter worked for me once, so I decided to take the same strategy.

Combined with continued curiosity on the CPG side of things, I accepted the role at Rubbermaid (to the surprise of some in my circles at Northwestern) and proceeded with a different kind of "Snap & Go" than I had ever known before.

Instead of snapping a football between my legs, I would be snapping food storage to stores across America. Or at least that's what I guessed at first—the reality was much more than totes and food storage, and again . . . less about the *what* and more about the *how* of this exciting new opportunity with a promising future.

I took the job. And after a few months of training, I was moved to my first real role based in Madison, Wisconsin. My core responsibility? Calling on 10 area-Walmart locations, supplying their shelves with Rubbermaid products, and coordinating with department managers on a daily basis.

I know, I know . . . to the untrained Tupperware eye, this might not seem so exciting to you. But for me, there was so much more than the job itself I found exciting, which mostly involved the wonderful people I got to work with day in and day out. We were a *team*, and I took the same strategy with me that I had learned years prior of working lock-step with a committed team toward a common goal.

That is why I think, in the remaining pages that follow, you will understand how a Snap & Go mentality applies to *whatever* your role and/or title is in the working world. From C-Suite executives to the maintenance team, from working moms to third shift workers, and from drive-thru cashiers to direct reports. The beginning of my career at Rubbermaid taught me *so much* about how I would approach the rest of my career:

• One's background doesn't matter nearly as much as the person in front of you today.

- Rapport with internal team members or external clientele is all about *rapport* built over an extended period of time.

- The trust that results from such rapport is what strong culture is made of, and it leads to teams that thrive.

- Thriving is crucial for every component of business—sales, HR, customer service, and leadership—and it starts with the mental and emotional health of each worker.

- And finally, hard work is the great separator between an average employee and an employee that is on his or her way to success.

Now, it's important to note I didn't say how hard work leads to climbing the ladder of success but simply success in itself.

It's important to make that distinction because success, for so long, was defined in our economy by climbing the ladder and making more money, earning a higher status, and attaining more power along the way. But that couldn't be further from the truth.

Some of the most successful people I met at Rubbermaid, especially earlier on in my career, are some of the most humble and hard-working individuals I've met to this day. They're the kind of workers I *loved* because I was cut from a similar cloth—a cloth that had direct ties to my time in the trenches . . . to my time rubbing shoulders with those who don't care about getting the credit, as long as we were winning the game.

But lest you think Rubbermaid consisted of a bunch of burly offensive-lineman types, I assure you . . . our team—those in the Phoenix Program and beyond—consisted of smiling faces and hard-working attitudes. Rubbermaid was built upon a "from the ground up" approach, where many of us knew each other's roles, and how we could fill the gaps when a gap was found. Yet another comparison to my time fighting on the offensive line.

All in it together. Nobody was complaining about credit. We weren't playing on the nation's biggest stage, but such is the case for most workers in America.

We had a chip on our shoulder, but it was the good kind—the same kind of chip that guys like Michael Jordan played with because when you feel like the world is counting you out, that's when some people decide to perform their best.

As I mentioned before, I had some friends from Northwestern question my decision to work at Rubbermaid instead of earning more money and prestige at a company in New York. Many years later, I don't blame them for their line of thinking . . . but I also don't have a single regret about launching my career alongside a winning team—even if they were labeled as "underdogs" at first.

In the end, America loves the underdog. The underdog is the one who checks entitlement at the door, and the underdog is the one who truly plays fearlessly. I know that a 6'7", 300 lb 24-year-old young man doesn't look like your typical "underdog" walking around Walmart stocking shelves, but it's the exact kind of mentality I loved playing with.

You see, when you're the underdog and not the top dog, you don't have as much pressure to do it all by yourself. Instead, you have no other choice but to rely on your team. And I promise you this . . .

The Snap & Go mentality is only as good as the team by your side.

9

When you make big life decisions, there will inevitably be other voices that want a say in the matter. Friends, family, and mentors . . . there are those that have their own view or opinion for the next step you might take in this life. And it takes some discernment to first acknowledge most of those people just want the best for you.

However, I recognize that sometimes you will ask for the opinions of others, and sometimes they will tell you their opinion *regardless* if you asked for it or not. No matter what camp these opinions are coming from, there is something crucial about the decision-making process: *you're* the one making the decision. Not them.

The first time I had to make such a decision was in high school—it was the time I had *a lot* of voices speaking about where I might attend college and play football. I'm lucky that most of my friends and family supported my decision no matter what, but having collegiate-level coaches and players try to entice you to their programs is an interesting process to be a part of, and can muddy the waters of one's decision.

It was the first time in my life I needed to learn how to quiet the noise around me and make the best decision with the choice (or set of choices) before me.

The years of preparation are there. The game is at hand. You spread your legs apart and stand over the prolate spheroid of leather. You place your hands on the football, appropriately interwoven with the laces.

Snap.

The ball soars backward and you explode from your stance, and look up at the scene ahead. For me, just like back at Happy

Valley, that's the best kind of silence there was—a silence that meant I did my job, and the rest was getting to cause some chaos and have some fun.

That silence is what you're after in the decision-making process.

The years of preparation are there. The game (read: choice) is at hand. You find a quiet spot at a park or near your home. You weigh all your options and take a deep breath. And all of the noise—thousands of screaming voices—simply *must* fade into the background or else you can't do your job well.

It obviously looks a little different in a football game than in real life, but the logic stands. Making a decision is all about tuning out the wrong voices, listening to the right ones, and in the end . . . making a decision you know to be right and true.

My decision to go work at Rubbermaid was the first real-world decision I needed to make, and because I had been through the college recruiting process, I had a little experience with weeding out the voices of those around me. In my gut, I felt this company was spearheading a promising future in an industry that really intrigued me. Before I knew it, I was living in beautiful Madison, Wisconsin, and working with some pretty amazing people. But even the best people in an amazing location doesn't mean doubt won't creep into the process . . .

Early on in my career with Rubbermaid, we were tasked with a specific amount of truckload sales to make each month. Each of these trucks contained between $12,000 and $15,000 of product on them, and those in my role were responsible for selling a truckload at a time to those area Walmarts we worked alongside. It was one of those moments I experienced doubt about the decision I had made—not because of my role or the company I was working for, but wondering if I was up for the challenge.

It was one of the first moments I also learned about *trust* in the sales process. Anyone you're selling to, *they're* in the decision-making seat and they won't decide to do anything with you if they don't trust you.

Therefore, I made sure that forming strong relationships preceded any of those truckload sales to our area stores.

When the week came to showcase our truckloads full of inventory, I approached each of the store managers I had spent months cultivating relationships with and working alongside—making lesser sales and carrying on with business as usual. But to sell that amount of product a truckload at a time? It was my hope and prayer that some of them said yes . . . and a few of them did! But the end result was not *nearly* close to the goal I had set for me.

Great . . . so I wasn't cut out for this gig.

The amount of time, energy, and effort I put into this specific task left me disappointed in the end, and the time came to report the earnings to the store director.

I walked into his office in Madison one day, showed him the results, and informed him about the excess inventory we now had on our hands . . .

Where do we go from here? What could I have done differently? Did I do something wrong or say the wrong thing?

I brought these kinds of questions to his office that morning, but it was his response that assured me of the decision I made after college—with this growing company and specific niche industry.

"Look here, Jack," the store director said, "we saw how hard you worked over the last few months. We don't care about the excess inventory—we'll figure out ways of getting the product moved. But what you and our other reps did was so much more important than sales. You guys built rapport with our associates and real-life customers that will certainly help us in the long run. You had fun doing it, laughed along the way, and brought energy into the store. That's what's important. We'll figure out the rest."

Is that quote word-for-word? No, but it's pretty darn close—because his response meant that much to me in that season of life. I was a 24-year-old kid in his first real-life job, and those words just totally lifted my spirits after I thought I massively failed.

It's the kind of encouragement from a boss or mentor that can obliterate thousands of doubts in your own mind, and thousands of outside voices saying, "Do it this way" or that way.

I'm not exactly sure why Rubbermaid called the program I joined after Northwestern the "Phoenix Program" but there is something cool I guess about the well-known phoenix that rises from the ashes. And even though I wasn't a college graduate that felt like I was emerging from an ash heap, I *was* a young kid on the brink of his career. For me, it was more about surrounding myself with the kind of people I wanted to become someday, and those kinds of early conversations with my director are what sealed the deal for me —the kinds of conversations that made any giant salary I would have made in New York a thing of the past.

From that moment in the store director's office, I was off to the races. It's like I could play free with what had been entrusted to me, and I no longer held myself to such high expectations—work simply became doing the best with whatever had been entrusted to me, and building strong relationships along the way.

That simple equation eventually set me up for an opening in Atlanta—where Rubbermaid is headquartered.

The new role was a Team Leader in Rubbermaid's southeast division, so I would be in charge of a dozen other sales reps, kind of like my old role in Madison—I was pumped! It was the first of my life experiences that led to a unique kind of opportunity: teach and train others on the Snap & Go mentality.

In other words, my time as a Team Leader in Atlanta was the first time in my life I got to teach the principles you've read about in this book—taking a simple action I had perfected throughout high school and college and applying that action to work and life.

Prepare. Evaluate. Execute.

If I had to boil it down to a work-related setting, I think those three words do a great job of encompassing the Snap & Go mentality. But there are three other words that I think go a layer deeper . . .

Humble. Hungry. Smart.

Before I type another word, please note those three words are derived from Patrick Lencioni's *The Ideal Team Player* is a book I have come to know well in the present day, but back then was just an idea I had to work off of from years as a collegiate athlete and young professional. If the Rubbermaid reps I was in charge of in Atlanta worked with humility, hunger, and a smart mind then they would be set up well to prepare, evaluate, and execute. That's it! Whether they failed or succeeded in the aftermath didn't matter —just like the store director in Madison told me.

It was fun working in that Team Leader role in Atlanta. But I wish I could say that sojourn lasted a little longer . . . I didn't even make it a full year before I was promoted to a job in a division I hadn't even thought of working in before at Rubbermaid within the greater Walmart ecosystem: cookware.

Cookware?!

I wasn't upset, but I was just confused about what I could bring to the table (no pun intended) since I, myself, was the farthest thing from a cookware expert. As a bachelor with a small Atlanta apartment, I knew I had a few pots and pans lying around but wasn't sure how I'd cultivate the kind of experience necessary to thrive in this new role.

But again, that was my *first* reaction before I quieted myself. Remember? The decision-making process is all about remembering what got you there in the first place, taking a deep breath, and finding a quiet place to gather your thoughts, make a decision and move full-steam ahead. In other words, the Snap & Go mentality in a nutshell.

When I took a step back, I was reminded that the decision really had nothing to do with cookware—it had *everything* to do with those three words from Lencioni on being a humble, hungry, and smart team player for the good of the overall vision.

The only caveat to this cookware position? It was located in Bentonville, Arkansas.

Bentonville, Arkansas?!

Similar to my "cookware" reaction was the Bentonville decision, but in the same way, I had to take a step back before accepting the role, I took a step back and gained a better perspective on this pending change in scenery—all with a little help from my father.

I was in Atlanta for 11 months before accepting the role and pending a move to Bentonville. I thoroughly enjoyed my time in Atlanta, and it's a place I have fond memories of to this day. Traveling west from Atlanta was a new experience for me, and it was a wonderful way to experience the beautiful American south. Still, I wondered if it was the right move for me at the time. Bentonville was the hot spot because of Rubbermaid's key initiatives alongside Walmart, and Bentonville is where Walmart is headquartered. If you know anything about Bentonville in the modern-day, you know there is some really great stuff happening there! But for a kid from Chicago, Bentonville might as well have been in South America.

Alright, so Bentonville isn't *that* south, but you get the idea.

On my way to Bentonville—all my things packed in the back of a U-Haul—I stopped at some random spot to eat along the way. And then I called my dad.

"Dad, I just am not sure what I'm doing—this move doesn't seem to make sense from a work or living point of view. I just don't know . . ."

It was the kind of cold feet doubt that accompanies most of us on the threshold of change. And it's the kind of doubt that runs counter to the way I kicked this chapter off —as I explained the necessity of shutting out the thousands of voices trying to sway you one way or another. In this case, I was running to one of those voices that I trusted most in my father, and his encouragement was just what I needed to hear before moving to an entirely new state and working in an entirely different area of business.

"Jack, you're gonna do great," my dad said, "And it's just another phase of your career— it's all an adventure. And my guess is that you're gonna meet a sweet, young, southern, co-ed down there."

At the core of that conversation with my dad was a calming presence that I needed at that time. He was the one to put me at ease, and it doesn't surprise me that he added that bit about finding a girl while in Arkansas. It's just funny now to look back on because that's exactly what happened.

When I drove over a giant hill in Arkansas, on Interstate 540, is when I saw the lights of a fun little college town in Fayetteville, Arkansas (near Bentonville). It was at that moment I realized everything was going to be OK. There *was* a civilization on the other end of the decision I had made, and there was no turning back now—my dad helped me see that's exactly where I needed to be.

On the other end of confidently making a decision is freedom. The freedom to sprint down the field and put trust in all the hard work you put in until that very moment.

10

There's a great scene from the movie *Top Gun*. And even though the sequel (2022) was an amazing flick, there's a nostalgia and "classic" element of the original (1986) that just can't be beat. The cheesiness. The music. And Tom Cruise and Val Kilmer in their prime. But there's a scene in that movie that is about as iconic as any from the 1980s.

Maverick and his wingman, Goose, are in a local bar with their Air Force buddies and have an eye out for women at the bar. But in the scene, Maverick locks eyes with *the* woman he wants to pursue. What follows is Maverick and Goose as wingmen but in a different context than flying—they team up to serenade Maverick's crush, and belt the song lyrics to *You've Lost That Lovin' Feelin'* by The Righteous Brothers. Classic!

With that scene in mind, I want to paint a similar picture in a similar bar outside of Fayetteville, Arkansas. Specifically, if you're familiar with Northwest Arkansas, you know that Dixon Street is the main artery through downtown Fayetteville and is frequented by college students attending the University of Arkansas nearby. Well, there are a number of young professionals who frequent those bars as well. Enter me and a few buddies I made at Rubbermaid during those first few months in my new role.

We were at one of those bars just hanging out—similar to Maverick and Goose—but were being serenaded by *someone else* through a loud microphone nearby. Turns out that "loud microphone" was the most beautiful voice I had ever heard. But she couldn't be that good-looking, could she? Well, she was. A "Miss Arkansas" beauty pageant participant to be exact. Seriously! I couldn't believe it but knew I somehow needed to channel my inner Maverick and talk to her.

She was absolutely stunning. Blonde, green eyes, and the epitome of a "southern belle." For this guy from Chicago's south side, I didn't exactly catch her attention in the way she caught mine. Nevertheless, with some liquid courage in my system, I approached her and complimented her on her voice. She said, "Thanks!" and got out of dodge. She wasn't prepared to strike up a conversation with a random stranger a few years older than her, but I *was* prepared to wait until she was ready.

Therefore, as my friends and I frequented the same bars over the next few months, I kept a keen eye out for the blonde with the beautiful voice, and on a cool fall evening . . . it happened. She returned the conversational favor, which led to exchanging phone numbers. Back in those days—the early 2000s—a phone number led to a phone call, and a phone call ideally led to a dinner date.

Our first dinner date occurred at Shogun in Fayetteville—a hibachi-style restaurant. While sitting near the hibachi grille that night, our chef watched as Erin and I got to know each other. But to him, it apparently looked like we had known each other for a while.

"How long have you two been married?"

I'm sure we both blushed a little before telling him it was our first date. But that moment proved something we both knew pretty early on—there was something special about our connection. It's the time in my life I was most grateful for Betty Harnedy's life example: the most important person in the room is the one in front of you.

When I was with Erin, that was easy. And for the months and years that would follow, Erin as the most important person in front of me has been the greatest honor of my life. More on our marriage and "present-day reality" a bit later, but here is the point in this book where I begin to land the Snap & Go plane.

It may seem like speeding up the story a bit, but make no mistake . . . meeting Erin and our dating relationship that followed feels like, in retrospect, the beginning of the rest of my life—in the most fun and exciting way possible.

Up until that point, Snap & Go was a mentality I had largely implemented in terms of my athletic and working career. But this third component I was about to embark upon was the area I was so excited to give my all. And when I say "give my all" I do mean "all in" on the love of my life.

Erin and I rode that hibachi moment for about nine months before I popped the question, and the girl who rightfully blew me off at a bar was now wearing a shiny new ring—all thanks to her fiance that eventually learned how to move some cookware.

Our big day was a glorious mix of southern glam and the best parts of a wonderful Chicago community. Between my family and Northwestern connections, we had a gorgeous Arkansas wedding. After years of competing in the southern beauty pageant circuit, Erin walked down the aisle as the most beautiful human I had ever seen on earth. What she physically saw in me—a big and tough collegiate offensive lineman—I'll never know . . . but I like to think I have other good qualities, and I'm grateful she was willing to take those along with a rough exterior.

Erin and I got married on July 9, 2005, and were ready to take on the world! Or at least Northwest Arkansas, which brings me back to moving cookware for Rubbermaid — something I *did* nail down after a brief learning curve when I first drove over from Atlanta. But the flip side of cookware coincided with some fun career development.

After working with Rubbermaid/Kimberly-Clark/Walmart for seven years, I got a position running our H-E-B Supermarkets team that took Erin and me to San Antonio, Texas. After a brief stint in San Antonio (three years) we were relocated to Cincinnati so I could run Kimberly-Clark's team for Kroger at the corporate office — an opportunity to lead a cross-functional team of about 30 wonderful people. Cincinnati was one final pit stop (before leading to our current location) where I met one of the more influential individuals in my life.

If you are a Nascar fan, you might recognize the name Tad Geschickter. Even if you aren't, fame and recognition is the last thing on Tad's mind. It's the reason I want to mention him as a leader in my life because it's his humility that is constantly in the back of my mind as I undertake any kind of leadership role. It's Cincinnatti where I first met Tad. These days, from time to time, we reconvene at the Atlanta Motor Speedway, where you can watch him in action as his team operates on the pit row.

I have seen Tad lead his Nascar team with grit and determination, but more than anything, I have watched him lead with humility at every step. To get an idea of the kind of guy Tad is, I once watched him fill in for a chef on their Nascar team who fell ill on race day. Not complaining about donning an apron during the festivities, Tad grabbed a spatula and started grilling out for all 30 team members and guests—myself included.

He's the standard, in my opinion, when it comes to leading a team with humility and fun in mind, but also excellence and empowering those around you to be better.

His is a relationship that made my work sojourn to Cincinnati worth it in itself.

But eventually, all roads lead back to my hometown. When an opportunity with Colgate-Palmolive was put on my radar, it wasn't an opportunity I was looking for at the time. But there were elements about the position I couldn't ignore, so I accepted a position at Colgate-Palmolive in their Chicago office, even though it would mean frequent travel to and from their New York headquarters.

In 1945, Betty and 'Red' Harnedy moved to Chicago to start a family and pursue their working dreams. In 2017, Erin and I did the same.

We knew Chicago had everything to offer that we desired in terms of raising our own children in a community that would be both familiar and supportive of us in the process. We love this city, and make frequent trips to Arkansas to visit her family. In (2014), our energetic son, Alec was born. And in (2017), our creative daughter, Elise followed her older brother.

In 1987, I was an elementary school kid riding in the backseat of our parent's Dodge Dart—my sister by my side. Time is a crazy thing, as Erin and I are now in the driver's seat, with brother and sister sitting behind us. But we wouldn't have it any other way.

As for work, I spent five wonderful years at Colgate-Palmolive. My time there actually had a pretty sweet ending, but more on that in a bit. For now, I want to transition into a crucial section of this book . . .

It was always my intention to write this book with *you* in mind and what you might take away from my story for the good of your own life, career, and legacy. We started this book with Chapter 1, and I detailed 10 specific steps of the long-snapping process. Since that moment in the book, I didn't really revisit those 10 steps . . . until now.

Because you might have missed it, each of the 10 chapters in this book actually resembles each of those steps—and a brief summation is how I'd like to round out this book, and set you off on your own Snap & Go journey.

1 | Play Like You Practice

Practice throughout the week prior.

In Chapter 1, I set the tone and objective of this book. Hopefully, in preparing you for the book itself, you were more ready to receive the pages that followed!

In life, you can't underestimate the power of practice. It's the number one thing that separates good players from great players, and how you approach the prep that goes into the game will define your life as well. Consider the following . . .

The average college football team will punt in a game around 50 times per season. Therefore, I made a total of 200 in-game snaps at Northwestern. Times that by an average of 10 seconds per play and that's 2,000 seconds . . . which equals 33 minutes of on-field playing time in a four-year career as a long snapper.

With that in mind (because I've done the math) consider the 21,600,000 seconds of practice/snapping/workouts over a five-year career (including my redshirt season) that equates to 360,000 minutes of practice. That number . . . all for 33 minutes of playing time.

Opportunities for practice are an *everyday* occurrence—it's just a matter of if you're willing to seek out and seize those opportunities.

2 | Use Your Senses

Visualize yourself playing in the game.

As a kid, you largely operate on senses because it's all you know of the world: what you see, hear, smell, taste, and touch.

For me, all those senses apply to a south side Chicago upbringing in which I can literally, if I close my eyes, see those streets and neighborhoods we'd drive down, hear the sounds of those streets but more importantly Bulls games on the radio, smell the Chicago steel industry in the air, taste my mother's cooking, and touch the fishing pole with my friends on a Saturday afternoon.

But it's how those senses apply to my parents and their leadership that stick with me the most—in addition to the love and support of my sister, Carrie!

Think about your own senses and how they apply to your upbringing: what did you see? Hear? Touch?

I heard and saw a loving marriage and a faithful sibling lay a firm foundation for the rest of our lives. But if your upbringing was a little more bleak, you have the opportunity to lay a similar foundation for future generations.

3 | Prepare with Faithfulness

Focus during pre-game.

Whether you caught it or not, the generational impact was a huge theme of this book. And, for me, I'd like to think it started with Betty and 'Red' Harnedy moving back to Chicago after World War II. However, I knew the roots of our Harnedy clan stretch way beyond the twentieth century. Specifically, I think about my own Harnedy and Dennehy ancestors living (to this day) in Ireland. I think about my great-grandmother's home in County Cork, Ireland—the little farmhouse she grew up in as a girl. My great-grandmother was just a girl when she'd walk a total of 12 miles to and from school every day. That kind of small faithfulness eventually led to generations after her. I am forever grateful for those Cork roots and the hard-working people there . . . just such a different life than we can think of in today's world, but I like to think of their grit that has remained in some way throughout our family lineage.

Regardless of your own family history, know that every decision you make in this life is paving the way for a generation to come. That generation *might* come within your own family line, but it also might just be for society at large.

What kind of foundation are you laying for those that come after you? A question to consider when preparing for tomorrow—I hope you prepare with faithfulness.

4 | Line Up Accordingly

Listen to your blocking assignment.

Alongside my best friend from high school, Kevin Dowling, we made a pretty good team on the offensive line together. But there were nine other guys we went to battle with on any given play, and we counted on each other to do our job for a common goal.

You can't line up accordingly at the beginning of a play if you don't know the people to your left and right and their respective roles on the field.

Who is on *your* team in life? Friends, family, and coworkers—all are a part of your team whether you realize it or not, but the extent to which you *know them* is up to you. I encourage you to make that extra effort to know them and their assignment in life, even if it means hopping in your car for a trip to Burrito Station. I promise burritos are a great way to bond.

5 | Scan the Defense

Strategize pre-play.

Chapter 5 was about the first time in life I had to strategize in regard to the next steps in life. Scanning the defense in football is the *result* of preparation before the game, but when it comes to making a decision . . . you need to know what you're up against.

Recognize the defense's soft spots and where they're weak. Once you identify and attain leverage, you can then pinpoint your next assignment and run toward it with everything you have. But not before a couple more steps in the process . . .

6 | Double-Check Your Surroundings

Look back at the punter to confirm he's ready.

Double-checking your surroundings is your last chance to recognize you're not alone before the play begins. For a long-snapper to check on the punter, you are acknowledging that your life is only a small part of a larger whole. Now, your role, although small in the grand scheme of things, is still VERY important for the execution of any given play.

Although my role was small at Northwestern University, I was affirmed that my role on the team *did* matter according to a much bigger vision for the future of the program.

Acknowledge your teammates and trust them to do their job—then there's only one thing left to do . . .

7 | Trust Yourself

Snap the ball blindly.

The "Snap" in Snap & Go is obviously about 50% of what it takes for a punt play to go according to plan. It's crazy that the motion happens blindly for a long snapper. But if you take the aforementioned six steps to heart, this seventh step is a lot less daunting than it may seem.

No matter your craft, the time and repetition you spend on that skill or set of skills *will* take care of itself come game time. All you need to do is trust the hours, days, weeks, months, and years of preparation prior.

8 | Fully Commit

Block a speedster rushing your gap.

Where all the preparation in the world leads to that one moment—your skill set on display—everything that comes after is encompassed on the "Go" side of things.

This is where the real fun comes into play because life is and should be . . . fun! Please, after you put this book down, don't take a second for granted. There is so much in this life to live for, and just being a part of the game is enough—but to *participate* in the action is a true gift.

After graduating from Northwestern, I knew I was entering the grind of my working career. But again, the grind felt more like a gift, and I chose to view it as such from day one. It just so happened to be with a great company and even better leadership that opened some cool doors for me! Identify those kinds of mentors in your corner, and run alongside them toward a common goal if you're lucky enough to get the chance.

9 | Leave It All Out on the Field

Sprint downfield with your head on a swivel.

Whether you have the opportunity to run alongside the best friends and co-workers in this life, or if you feel isolated on the road to success . . . all you can control is *yourself* in the process. And if you take that truth to heart, then you can follow this simple rule:

Leave it all out on the field.

When the final whistle blows, and it will blow for each one of us, men and women will gather at your funeral, and I hope and pray that this occasion is more of a time to celebrate who you were at your core, and not just people making things up about someone they didn't know. I know it might sound intense, but the fact of the matter is I've attended multiple funerals in my life, and I've experienced both of those kinds of occasions.

I have experienced funerals where nobody really knew the person who died because he or she was kind of standoffish, even if they were a great person at their core. But I've also attended funerals like my best friend, Kevin Dowling, my uncle Bill Harnedy, and Uncle Joe. Both of those individuals, as sad as their funerals were, was also a time to celebrate two men who left everything they had on the field.

Live your life in such a way, and I promise the last event of your life will be a celebratory one among people whose life you impacted greatly.

Note: There are more in my life I know who experienced an earlier whistle: Kristin, Craig, Matt H, Leon, Bobby "Fluff", Rashidi, and Matt P. And I'm sure that, sadly, you have your own list of people who left this world too soon. Consider them when you put this book down shortly and how you might honor their lives accordingly with a Snap & Go mentality.

10 | Execute the Opportunity

Locate and tackle the ball carrier.

Execution is the word this book has been working toward all along. Why? Because you can only read so much about one guy's story and perspective before going out and living out *your* story and journey. Trust me when I say I can't wait to hear it! I encourage you to reach out to me at jackharnedy.com with how the Snap & Go mentality affects your life.

The last thing I'll say about execution is that it starts with repetition—like standing in your driveway as a goofy teenager, bent over a football and flinging it against the wall 1,000+ times or to your dad in the backyard in the pouring down rain or inches of snow, before it's something you could do with your eyes closed. But that's just one example. Here are a few more:

- Selling a product you believe in.

- Mentoring someone younger than you.

- Taking your spouse out for date night.

- Attending your kids' events.

- Hitting your work-related goals.

- Encouraging a coworker.

- Serving your community.

- Donating to a cause.

Repetition in any of these areas is how they become more than commonplace, but a ritual that has the power to change the world—one person in front of you at a time.

This book was 10 seconds of an average punt play that represented each chapter, and 10 chapters that speak to the 10 core principles of this Snap & Go mentality I now entrust to you no matter where you're at in your own life and leadership journey.

If you've made it this far in the book, I want to say THANK YOU first of all because there are a lot of great business and leadership books out there, and at the end of the day, I'm just an average guy with a lucky upbringing who is trying to bestow the wisdom I learned onto a new generation.

You might be my age or older. That's great! Join me in handing this Snap & Go mindset down to younger generations that are going to build the future. You might be a young professional like I was once upon a time, stacking Walmart shelves with the best

Rubbermaid supplies money can buy. Stay curious early in your career, and trust the preparation that got you to where you are today. The rest is just going out there and doing what you were born to do, and most importantly loving others well along the way.

No matter your age, I'm reminded of what makes football so great: it's a game. And no matter your favorite sport, it's just a game. But life is similar. We're all given an opportunity to play this game, and we get the choice of how hard we'll pursue the goal line in front of us. For me, I only knew one speed toward the goal line—and for a 6'7" kid from south side Chicago, it may not have been *as fast* as I thought it to be. But in my mind, I was going to give everything I had to put one step in front of the other.

In those 10 seconds, you'll hear a lot of noise. In those 10 seconds, others will be aiming to knock you down. But in those 10 seconds, you have a shining opportunity to make a difference in the game. Seize that opportunity. Seize *any* opportunity you've been given today to make a difference. That's how Kobe did it. That's how Michael did it.

But as for me, I've always been more inclined to that prolate spheroid of leather.

So throw on your helmet and pads and don't take a second for granted. The final whistle might blow at any moment.

I know you're more than ready to take the field.

AFTERWORD

Earlier in the book, I mentioned how the end of my time working at Colgate-Palmolive had a pretty sweet ending . . .

Well, that's because I ended up taking a job at Hostess Brands as their Senior Director of Revenue Growth Management. What started as trying out Rubbermaid's Phoenix Program eventually led to leading a wonderful team as we supply the world with one of the world's best-known snacks and/or indulgences—take your pick.

But whether your title is similar to mine as "Manager" or "Director" or even "Entry Level", know that your position on the field *is* more than necessary for our team to succeed. And when I say "team," I mean society at large . . . starting with your own family and rippling out into your local community.

Once you put this book down for good, promise me you'll view every day as an opportunity to step onto the field and make a difference. Anything less is not squeezing the most out of your own God-given ability.

That ability is inside of you. Whether the world is ready for you or not, it's time to Snap & Go with everything you have—I hope you cause some chaos in the process. And I hope that chaos is covered in kindness.

ACKNOWLEDGMENTS

Writing this book has been an amazing journey. Tapping deep into memories and experiences and it could not have turned into a reality without the help from Streamline Books. Will Severns, you are an amazing person. You could pull "it" out of me when I didn't think it was there. I am honored to have had the time with you, and I am grateful to call you friend. Allison Lewis, your attention to detail and encouraging words along the way made this possible. Trevor Waite, for keeping our project on time and on task. And to Alex Demczak—it's amazing how far one LinkedIn message can go. You have a great message and vision and I love what you are building.

This book has been an accumulation of my life experiences and the lessons along the way. So many people have influenced and played a major role in my life that I simply cannot thank everybody by name. BUT, there are several people that deserve special recognition and a big thank you for all you have done directly or indirectly for my life and career . . .

To my wife, Erin. Your love and support for the last 17+ years has been unwavering. I love the journey we are on together. Thank you for always pushing me to do and give my best, even if it means it takes me away from the family all too frequently. I never have to worry about keeping the household together as I know you are always in charge and steps ahead of me. You always keep me grounded, and remind me to never get "too big for my britches." You tell me like it is, and expect the same back . . . and you do it in a fun-loving, happy, and carefree way.

I love watching you connect with everybody you encounter, no matter who they are. You can quickly build a connection with anybody in a meaningful way, and that has enabled us to have many amazing and long-lasting friendships.

Your interior design "eye" is a tribute to your creativity and it's a gift that needs to be shared more! We are the benefactors! Having a beautiful environment at home helps all of us. I am excited that you will have some more time now that the kids are getting older to be able to share your art & craft with friends and clients.

You are raising two amazing children, and they are fortunate to call you Mom, and I am proud to be your husband!

To my son, Alec, and daughter, Elise. You embody the best parts of your mom and me. We love you so much and are so lucky to have two creative, hard-working, spirited, and loving children. This book is for you. It's purposely written to not include much of our time together. We're building the chapters in the next book, together. Alec, you have the competitive spirit that will get you so far in life and I commit to always saying yes to going outside and playing catch, basketball, football, or doing your homework! Elise, I love your creative ways through art and dance. I will never turn down a chance to play with your animals or in your kitchen. To you both, play between the bell/whistle—give it your all, always in everything you do. Your Mom and I are here to support you through it all. You have all of our hearts.

To Carrie Harnedy Curran. Riley and Tommy are such special children. They are learning from a strong-willed, smart, and passionate Mom. I'll never forget you saying, "Thank you" to me for enabling you the opportunity to go to a "more expensive" university because of my scholarship. The humility you showed then and all through your life stood out then and does today.

To Grandma Doris and Grandpa Irv. You are always in my thoughts and prayers. You were always there for us with a big smile on your face. Your time with us was too short, but I know you both lived wonderful lives, and that lives through Pam, Karen, Mel, and Jeff.

To my extended family, cousins (Mike, Lisa, Chris, Bill, Angela, Maura, Mark, Kate, and Kevin), aunts (Maureen, Pam, Melanie, Lynne, and Meyra), and uncles (Bill, Joe G, Joe B, Kevin, and Jeff), your support through my life journey is truly appreciated. I loved coming out of the locker room at NU with a huge crowd waiting . . . for the Long Snapper!

To my special friends, I've been fortunate to have along the way, old and new. Thank you. I love picking up the phone or texting. Near or far, we pick up right where we left off.

To the Dowling Family. Know that Kevin's short life has impacted so many people over the last 25+ years. You would be proud to know that Kevin's legacy lives on. I hope this book is a small tribute to his life. He loved his brother, sisters, Mom, and Dad very much.

To all my coaches, Frank Lenti (Mt. Carmel Head Coach and all-time winning football coach in Illinois—attention to detail), Gary Barnett (Northwestern Head Coach— setting a vision and making it achievable), Randy Walker (Northwestern Head Coach —hard work and discipline), Greg Brandon (recruiting me to Northwestern), Tom Bratton (O-line coach at Northwestern— focus, and accountability), Jeff Genyk (Northwestern Special Teams coach - pursuing a career you're passionate about), and many others—thank you for helping me understand the importance of paying attention to every detail, repetition, forming good habits, performing your best every play, and reminding me to look forward. Keep the blinders on and focus on the next play and don't look back, unless it's in a film session where you can learn from your performance.

To the kickers, punters, and holders. Tim, Brian, Eron, JJ, JJ (yes two JJs), and Corb. The endless hours of practicing together. You helped me keep a level head. We cheered for each other when things were great, and we lifted each other up when somebody faced a challenge. We are a unique crew, and perform some of the most important plays during a game. We're expected to perform our best every play, no wonder they call it "special" teams.

To Tony Dunning. Thank you for being a great leader, mentor, spiritual "guide" and friend. You have taught me SO much about how to build a customer relationship. Your "Onward Always, Backwards Never" message still resonates with me today. I love our conversations and your impact on the CPG world is far greater than you take credit for.

Mel Bomprezzi, "Relationships are important, and this is a relationship business, Jack"—I will never forget our conversation in Daytona at the "restaurant" (Ok . . . "bar") at Hammock Beach. That conversation was the start of something special, and something amazing. I cherish our time together in Germany—where we turned our relationship from business partners to friends. Please know that you had a major influence on who I am today.

I have had the opportunity to work with some amazing leaders (direct managers) in the Consumer Packaged Goods industry. Drew, Josh, Dennis, Arist, Jim, Brian, and Philip, thank you for having faith in me to drive some of our companies' biggest businesses. Each of you brought a different leadership style, and I am an accumulation of you.

To all the Merchants at some of this country's biggest retailers, wow. You pushed me and my company to be better and always put the shopper first. We had many challenging conversations, but each and every conversation was rooted in respect for each other, and we always found a way to make the most of every opportunity. From growing up in the stores, to agreeing to very complex negotiations, I am forever grateful for our time together. Again, you all made me better. I smile at the many stories and memories I have of our meetings. So many good stories—maybe that's book #3?

To Jen Caballero. You are an amazing person—I love watching you push the norms in everything you do. You keep me grounded, and you are my first call/text in the morning to check in on your workout at Orangetheory Fitness. You're my accountability buddy, always have been, and always will be. I will always cherish our time in NY together, especially during the year I commuted back and forth. YOU made it fun and worthwhile. You will continue to do great things in our space, and well beyond.

Monica, what can I say? We have been through SO much together. The good and the bad, you always were the person I could turn to so that we could find the good in every situation. I value your strong opinions, the way you are able to communicate, and how you never back down. Your boys are so fortunate to have you as a role model. You and Josh are raising two grounded, happy, and hard-working kiddos. I have become a better person because of our friendship.

Jon Gordon, Patrick Lencioni, and Bethany Frankel. All authors that have been my fuel, especially over the last couple of years. Jon Gordon, I know you speak a lot about influencing, one person at a time. Please know that your messages, podcasts, emails, etc all were used by me to keep my 30-40 person team at Colgate-Palmolive inspired and engaged throughout the pandemic (and beyond). Your Power of Positive Leadership is and always will be the best training somebody who aspires to be a leader could attend.

Patrick, I met you years ago at a conference, and you were so welcoming and treated me like I was the only person in the room . . . sound familiar? Thank you!

Bethany, your speech at the Nielsen Annual Conference in Orlando in 2022 inspired me more than I could have ever expected. Your speech and your book gave me the courage I needed to make a big career change, thank you. And to think I was going to skip your talk during the conference. Goes to show you that you never know when and where you'll find your inspiration.

ABOUT THE AUTHOR

Jack Harnedy has worked in the Consumer Packaged Goods industry for the past 21 years across multiple functions and has worked with some of the largest and most well-known household brands. He is passionate about delivering growth, building strong teams, and doing it in a positive way. He lives just outside of Chicago with his wife and two children.

For his message on positivity, leadership, and what makes a team great, reach out to Jack on his website jackharnedy.com for more information on speaking engagements and bringing the Snap & Go mentality to life at your organization, company, school, or community.

Made in the USA
Coppell, TX
26 November 2022